WAIFS & STRAYS

OF

CELTIC TRADITION

LORD ARCHIBALD CAMPBELL

KNIGHT'S TOMB, ORONSAY CHAPEL
From a drawing by William Galloway

WAIFS AND STRAYS

OF

CELTIC TRADITION

I.

ARGYLLSHIRE SERIES.

Edited

With Notes on the War Dress of the Celts,

BY

LORD ARCHIBALD CAMPBELL.

First published in 1889 by David Nutt

This edition by Akerbeltz Publishing 2022

British Library Cataloguing-in-Publication Data.

A catalogue record for this book is available from the British Library.

ISBN 978-1-907165-53-5

PREFACE

These Tales open with contributions from three reverend gentlemen belonging to the Church of Scotland, all of them accomplished Gaelic scholars, namely, the Reverend D. MacInnes, than whom no better Celtic scholar could be named, nor one more capable of extracting the ore from that rich mine of hidden wealth, the traditions of the people of the country among whom he lives and by whom he is much beloved.

The same applies to the Reverend Jas. McDougall Dùrar, Ballachulish, Appin, whose charge lies close to the solemn glen made famous by the inhuman massacre of Glencoe.

It will be acknowledged that the fairy tale supplied by the Reverend Duncan M. Campbell of Tynribbie, Appin, is of great quaintness, for the rapid flight of the Highlander to Rome beats the performances of the famous Peter Schlemihl. The questions put by "Finn", or "Fionn", and the answers supplied by the ready "mother-wit" of the maiden, were sent by Mr. George Clark, head-keeper at Roseneath, who lived in former years in Glen Shira, near Inverary, and who is a Highlander, a man whose heart and soul lay in his profession. When in his prime, the boldest poacher of the Clydeside thought twice before coming to grips with this man, whose stern face and flashing eye reminds one of the description given by Scott of the Covenanter. He thought little, gun in hand, and his trusty dog by his side, of emerging from the sombre pine woods, and tackling any boat landing, no matter how dark the night, or how far from help he might be. Some tales I have been unable to include in this series, to my regret, but I hope, in a second and later series, to include what I am unable to publish now.

Without plunging into the abyss of Ossianic controversy – for there will, perhaps, be many, in the years to come, who will read Macpherson's *Ossian*, believing that the poems he gave out were handed down in that shape - I will give, in one sentence, the opinion of the late Campbell of Islay on this point, than whom no one was better fitted to judge.

In a letter dated July 3, 1881, Niddry Lodge, Kensington, he says: "*I am not thanked for* proving *MacPhersons* Ossian *to be his compositions, founded upon old heroic ballads.*"

I could now, with ease, get poems, *a la* MacPherson's Ossianic poetry, written out by certain Highland gentlemen, "founded on heroic ballads". Most publishers would demur to publishing any more Ossianic poetry, however. Campbell of Islay valued true translation of the Gaelic Tales and Poems, collected by Mr. Peter Dewar, and done into English by Mr, Hector Maclean, more than volumes of Macpherson, and so would most, if not all, Gaelic scholars.

The notes on Celtic war dress are given as a contribution to the question as to what the garb of the Highlander was langsyne.

A. C.

CONTENTS

ILLUSTRATIONS

INTRODUCTION

WHENEVER Walter Scott launched one of his deathless works on an astonished world, many, both in this and in more distant countries, were eager to make closer acquaintance with the land that furnished such splendid material to his glowing pen, and neither the rain, nor mist, nor angry seas have been able to damp the ardour of his admirers.

His readers for generations to come will probably visit the scenes made romantic by his pen. Be it his wondrous prose, or the fiery lines of poetry, which are ever recurring to the mind as we sweep past the mountains or the islands of the West. Close study will show what the state of the Highlands was. In the rude days there was plenty wherewithal to weave, to a mind such as his, a web of splendid fiction.

Deeds of daring are common, deeds of violence more so. Passionate love-tales abound. The very depths of devotion appear to be reached in the commonest narration of the "following" of the chieftain, who seldom hesitated to place their lives as forfeit for the master. One of the great links between the nobles and gentry generally and the people was the system of fosterage, by which the very characters of the children of the richer class became imbued with the traits of the lower orders, with their mode of life and their thoughts. These were the rivets in the armour of the Highlanders, the rivets of love – none stronger could be forged. Were we to judge of the Highlands from the tales that have been laboriously gathered by trustworthy Celtic scholars, were we to judge impartially, we should be forced to acknowledge a country denuded to an astounding extent of law and order. What wonder that when certain families produced some master mind, some born ruler of men, who "forced the fighting" or kept the peace, that the Executive, who could not get at these wild regions, gratefully acknowledged such service to the State, and rewarded such men with lands, forfeit to the Crown for some signal act of violence or bloodshed? Such men *did* appear at various periods, and had it not been for them, the Highlanders would have long since been exterminated through internecine warfare and battle.

Again, when some great man appeared, the weaker septs of a clan readily adopted his name and, for lands granted, came out in war time under one banner. Such men – men who created an oasis of comparative peace – were the saviours of Scotland.

The calmness of the "follower" who executes a savage murder early one morning, in order to save his master the trouble, is typical of the spirit of the Highlander, whose conscience lay in acting faithfully in all things towards his chief. The extraordinary traits shown in tales such as the following are the same as were shown in later centuries towards Prince Charles Edward. The man who could butcher another to save his master the danger he might possibly run, is the same man – or the breed is the same – that spurned the gold offered for the betrayal of an unfortunate prince. They could commit the most cruel and ghastly murder, and yet be full of sentiment and tender feeling. These memorable traits should be remembered when dealing with the Celtic race, for the blood contains to this day the same characteristics, the same elements, discordant as they are – battle and murder and tender love.

The Celt of Ireland and the Celt of Western Scotland were in close and perpetual commune, and, until the days of the Reformation came, there were few events stirring Ireland that did not also, in a measure, stir the Western Highlands of Scotland. Peace was oftenest obtained in the Highlands by the fiery arbitrament of war. It took centuries to settle the southern district of Kintyre, and it was done at last by the introduction of Lowlanders. Such was the eloquent tribute paid to the latter by one of the ablest men of the 17th century – namely, Archibald Campbell, Marquis of Argyll.

It is true that he gave them the land because they were persecuted elsewhere, but he probably thought a leaven of Lowland blood would be conducive to the prosperity of the country.

It may be that Scott, when he wrote about the sorrows and sufferings of Captain Dugald Dalgetty, had another and a true incident in his head as to the treatment of a messenger who landed at Inverary and brought the grim Marquis a message. It is on record that on a certain occasion a messenger did land from a boat near to the Castle, and was promptly hit on the head by one of the Marquis' retainers, who probably thought that was only proper and right. The messenger, smarting from the blow, when he finally did get to the interview, complained of the way he had been treated – namely, struck over the head on landing. The answer of the Marquis was significant enough. Whether he felt the same irritation that exasperated his retainers or not is uncertain, but, for all answer, "he left the room, banging the door violently after him." Now that is not poetic, but probably exceedingly true to the life, and it may well have given Scott an invaluable clue to the manner of dealing affected by the great Marquis. So rough did this messenger consider the inhabitants that he got into the boat, grateful enough to receive no more blows! When a man could be thus treated when acting as a messenger to the great Marquis of Argyll, small as the incident may seem, it throws a flood of light on the unceremonious ways of those days.

Modern research in the Highlands leads us to give episodes as they happened, without gilding and varnishing the picture at all. When the Athol people "made a stable of Inverary", as Islay used to say, what is the first episode we know of? Sixteen gentlemen are hanged as a beginning, and the famous list of "Depredations" committed is a continuation. Not a cow or a horse remains, nor a shawl or a petticoat is left, clocks, all disappear into Athol arms, plaids – "Hieland" plaids and "Lowland" – all are taken. It would be difficult to wax romantic over the desolation, or the absurd load of goods the Athol men took on their backs, or the feasts they made on the heather on the captured cattle. Scott would have given us a brilliant volume, and he would doubtless have made the Athol man die another death than that recorded – namely, entering a house near Inverary during the raid, and drinking so much milk that, falling on the threshold coming out, he burst!

"Mine own romantic land" was far from a land of romance to those who had to live through those rough times, when men made howling wildernesses of the neighbour's lands, and a place of desolation for the wretched people to dwell in. The condition of the people was one of great discomfort, perpetual foray, and constant war. Their halcyon days were few indeed! The land of romance was one which only the very young and ignorant could venture to imagine themselves to be in. Let us continue to read the glorious romance of Scott, tempered every now and then with a glance at the Highlands as they really were – full of storms of all sorts.

That lovely land, fringed with idyllic woods and watered by the glorious lakes, will remain for all time ideal, but the real history of the land is one which presents much that is terrible and miserable to our gaze.

ARCHIBALD CAMPBELL.

Craignish Tales

The following traditions are connected chiefly with the "House of Craignish" (Taigh Chraiginis). This house was one of the oldest branches of the House of Loch Awe, which afterwards become that of Argyll.

The founder of the Craignish family was Dugald Campbell, who, by his marriage with the daughter and heiress of McEachern, inherited Craignish Castle and the lands attached to it. This, according to tradition, happened about the end of the 12th century. Dugald's descendants held the lands of Craignish down to the 16th century at least, when a failure took place in the direct male line, and the estate passed, it is thought, though there seems to be no documentary evidence for the supposition, to a collateral line. The new line continued in possession of Craignish up to the beginning of the present century, when the estate passed into other hands.

As one might expect from the antiquity of the House, and their isolated and exposed position on the west coast, their long history furnished abundant material for a large and varied stock of local traditions. These traditions were remembered, and widely known in the district during the first half of the present century. But, owing to a variety of causes, including the change in the tastes and habits of the present generation, traditions and tales of all sorts are no longer told, and are consequently forgotten. The following are only a very few remembered out of the many current in the parish upwards of forty years ago.

Craignish, like many other districts in the Highlands, had its storytellers. These belonged to a family of McLartys, once resident in Gartcharran, on the estate of Craignish Castle. Two members of the family, uncle and nephew, were remarkable for their knowledge of so-called Ossianic poetry. The former, Alastair MacTain, died about the end of the last century, and the latter, Alastair Tàillear, about fifty years ago. From the younger, the Rev.

Mr. Stewart, minister of Craignish, got the greater part of his collection of ancient poetry, and to the elder both the Rev. J. Smith, D.D., of Seann Dàna fame, and Mr. Duncan Kennedy, were indebted for a considerable proportion of the poems in their collections. Kennedy, in his collection of "Hymns and Spiritual Songs", says, in speaking of the elder McLarty, that "he could recite more of the poems of Ossian than any other person the editor had met with between the Mull of Kintyre and High Bridge in Lochaber." It was from a later generation of the same McLartys that all the following traditions were taken, except the Glengarrisdale tale, which was received from a Jura man, John MacFarlane, constable at Ballachulish.

The first tradition, the subject of which is the visit of Dugald Campbell's son to Innischonnell, and its consequences, belongs to the 13th century. MacMartin, whose name figures so prominently in the narratives, was, I am now told by two intelligent Loch Aweside men, the chief of the Clan McCorquodale. This account is most likely correct, as it is pretty certain that the McCorquodales lived at Fincharn long before they removed to the north end of Loch Awe, where they latterly resided. MacMartin must therefore have been the patronymic, and not the surname, of the person so designated in the tale. The *Gillean Maola Dubha* were the lowest class of retainers who hung about a chief's castle. They were called *Gillean Dubha* (utter, or out-and-out servants), from the servile work which they were called upon to perform, and *Maola*, not because they were *bald*, as the term might be translated, but from their habit of going always about *bare-headed*. In the time of peace they were the mere drudges of the castle, but when hostilities broke out between their master and his neighbours, they were among the first to follow him to the field, and among the bravest in the combat. Notwithstanding, they were usually nothing more than a parcel of idle and quarrelsome fellows, and the reluctance of Campbell in allowing them to accompany him to Loch Awe proceeded solely from fear lest they should create a disturbance on the way, or during his stay at Innisconnell.

Here are a few older tales than the Clan traditions which follow them.

The Fight between Bran and Foir or For.[1]

The black dog, Foir, was the brother of Bran, the far-famed hound of Fionn. Foir was taken early from his dam, and was afterwards nurtured by a band of fair women, who acted as his nurses. He grew up into a handsome hound, which had no equal, in the chase or in fight, in the distant North. His owner, Eubhan Oisein, the black-haired, red-cheeked, fair-skinned young Prince of Innis Torc (Orkney?), was proud, as well he might be, of his unrivalled hound. Having no further victories to win in the North, his master determined to try him against the strongest dogs in the packs of the *Fèinne*. He left home, descended by Loch Awe, and entered Craignish through Glen Doan. Before his arrival, the *Fèinne*, after spending the day in the chase, encamped for the night in the upper end of Craignish. Next day Fionn arose before sunrise, and saw a young man, wrapped in a red mantle and leading a black dog, approaching towards him at a rapid pace.

The stranger soon drew near, and at once declared his object in coming. He wanted a dog-fight, and so impatient was he to have it, and so restless by reason of his impatience, that he suffered not his shadow to dwell a moment on one spot. Fifty of the best hounds of the *Fèinne* were slipped at last, but the black dog killed them all one by one. A second and then a third fifty were uncoupled, but the strange dog disposed of them as easily as he did of the first.

---

1 Campbell of Islay, at page 92, *Leabhar na Fèinne*, says the name of the black dog, "For", means literally a "dog who would go far and near to get venison and prey for himself" – *A' forradh na leacainn* (ranging the hillside for food). Islay also refers to "Kennedy's 1st Collection, p. 48, Advocates' Library, Dec. 5, 1871", concerning this tale.

Fionn now saw that all the dogs of the *Fèinne* were in serious danger of being annihilated, and therefore he turned round and cast an angry look on his own great dog Bran. In a moment Bran's hair stood on end, his eyes darted fire, and he leaped the full length of his golden chain in his eagerness for the fight. But something else besides the casting of an angry look was still to be done to rouse the fierce hound's temper to its highest pitch. He was placed nose to nose with his rival, and then his golden chain was unclasped. The two hounds, brothers by blood, but now champions on opposite sides, at once closed in deadly fight, but for an adequate description of the struggle between them the reader must consult the bards. See the "Lay of the Black Dog", in Islay's *Leabhar na Fèinne*, the McCallum's *Ancient Poetry*, etc.

The contest lasted from morning to evening, and victory remained, almost to the close, uncertain, but in the end Bran vanquished Foir, and, by killing the latter, amply revenged the death of the three fifties. The *Fèinne* buried their own dogs, and the stranger, with a sore heart, laid his black hound in the narrow clay bed.

This great dog-fight, so celebrated in Gaelic lore, is said to have been fought at Lergychony, in Craignish. It is further said that the place was called *Learg a' Choinnimh*, or the "Plateau of Meeting", because it was there the two hounds met in fight. There are, of course, many other places in the Highlands which claim the honour of being the scene of this legendary contest. Among these is Dunmore, on West Loch Tarbert, with its *Dùn a' Choin Duibh*, where the dead hounds of the *Fèinne* are said to have been buried.

[Translated by the Rev. D. MacInnes.]

How Bran killed the Black Dog.

1. A day when we were in the hunting hill,
(We would deem it a loss to be without dogs)

Listening to the screaming of birds
And to the roaring of deer and elks.

2. We made slaughter there (without using stratagems)
With our venomous dogs and arms,
And came to our house in the afternoon
Cheerily, tunefully, and good-humouredly.

3. That night in Fionn's house,
Alas! merry men were we [2]
While we played instrumental music,
And consumed birds, deer, and elk.

4. Next day, Fionn rose early
Ere the sun rose on his dwelling.
And he saw, coming from the plain,
A man with a red garment and a black dog.

5. His appearance was as follows:
His cheek was of the berry's hue.
And his skin was whiter than moss-cotton,
Though his hair happened to be black.

6. The fine lad, whose head was stately like the elk's.
And on whose countenance no fear would lie.
Came to us to his great grief.
Demanding a fight of dogs.

7. At the beginning of the fight we let loose
The best dogs we had in our dwelling.
Fiercely fought the black dog.
And he killed three fifty dogs.

8. It was then that Fionn said,
"This is a hard and destructive fight";

---

[2] Ossian is looking back regretfully on the former flourishing condition of the *Fèinn*.

He turned his back on the people.
And looked with a frown on Bran.

9. Then Bran shook his gold chain:
His wailing was loud among the people:
His two eyes kindled in his head;
And he bristled up, eager for battle.

10. "Let the thong be loosed off my dog,
Whose deeds have hitherto been valiant.
And let us see a fair fight
Between Bran and the black dog."

11. They set the dogs nose to nose;
Among the people they shed blood.
There was a hard and fierce struggle
Before Bran killed the black dog.

12. "Man that hast come to our Fèinn,
As we have killed thy dog
Tell us thy name and surname.
And the land whence thou hast come,"

13. "Eibhinn Oisean is my name.
From King Torc . . . .
I never thought that there was among the Fèinn
Any dog that could wound For.

14. "Except Geòla with her wiles.
And Bran with his great strength.
There was not a dog fastened with a thong
In your tower my noble dog would leave alive.

15. "The shape of my dog was good.
The joint of his neck was far from his head,
Broad was his middle and broad his chest.
Bent was his fore-leg[3] and crooked his hind-leg.

---

3 *Lit.* elbow.

16. "Bran had yellow paws,
Two black flanks and a white belly,
A green back under which game would lie.
And two sharp, erect red ears.

17. "There is many a fair and pretty maiden.
Of bluest eye and golden hair.
In the country of the son of King Torc,
Who would give food to my dog to-night."

18. Then the true, generous hero,
Buried his dog in a narrow clay bed,
And the Fèinn also buried
In the mound westward three fifty dogs.

19. Eibhinn Oisean departed from us,
Regretting that he had ever come.
For he lost his good dog.
Which was of great intelligence, vigour, and strength.

20. MacCumhail of the gold cups
Had a thousand twenties of his fine army,
On the day when Bran killed the dog.
Playing and drinking in his tower.

21. Believe, Pàdraig, that it is true
That we had at one time great fame.
Though I am to-night, Clerk,
A poor, lonely visitor in your abode.[4]

---

[4] Few people realise that the mode of reciting Ossianic poetry was by acting the scenes. Clark, who refutes Shaw's attacks on the authenticity of MacPherson's poems, declared that he and MacPherson were present at wakes held in Badenoch, where Ossianic poems were recited and scenes acted by persons who made it a custom to recite these deeds of valour on great occasions. It is said that the generous phrases and moving language recited had a visible effect on the fiery and warm-hearted nature of the actors and reciters, and that they fairly caught the fire of the poetry which they were declaiming. (See Logan's *Gael*, vol. ii, p. 24.) In MacPherson's day the Highlanders still wore the ancient garb, and it must have been a strikingly picturesque sight to witness such a performance,

The Battle between the Craignish People and the Lochlainnich Norwegians at Slugan.

The Norwegians once made a sudden descent from their ships on the lower end of Craignish. The inhabitants, taken by surprise, fled in terror to the upper end of the district, and halted not until they reached the slugan (gorge) of Gleann Domhain, or the Deep Glen. There, however, they rallied under a brave young man, who threw himself at their head, and slew, either with a spear or an arrow, the leader of the invaders. This inspired the Craignish men with such courage that they soon drove back their disheartened enemies across Barbreck river. The latter, in retreating, carried off the body of their fallen leader, and buried it afterwards on a place on Barbreck farm, which is still called Dùnan Amhlaigh, or Olav's Mound. The Craignish men also raised a stone at Slugan to mark the spot where Olav fell.

The Hoof-prints of Scota's Steed at Ardifour Point.

At the mouth of Loch Craignish, but on the Kilmartin side of the loch, is the farm of Ardifour. One side of this farm faces Loch Craignish, and another Loch Crinan. Between the two lochs is a point where there are deep indentations in the rock, which bear some remote resemblance to the hoof-prints of a horse. How were these formed? A geologist could easily answer the question, but legend also has its own way of solving the difficulty. Scota, the daughter of Pharaoh, King of Egypt, came over from Ireland, and having entered the mouth of Loch Crinan, drew up her ship opposite Ardifour Point. She then mounted her steed, shook the reins, and thus urged the high-mettled animal to spring from the deck on to the distant point, and so violent was the shock that the

---

lit by the blazing peat and wood fire, aided by the ancient lamps that they had. – A.C.

hoofs of the horse sank deeply into the rock, and left behind them those marks which are still to be seen at Ardifour.

The Campbells were supposed to have come into possession of Craignish about the end of the 12th or beginning of the 13th century. This note is added by the Reverend James McDougall.

The editor fervently hopes that in the narration and publication of these tales offence is given to no one bearing the names herein named. Family folk-lore must ever be carefully dealt with, and a hard matter to relate at best.

A hearty apology is herewith tendered to anyone who feels in any way that the tales reflect unpleasantly on his or her forbears.

Small though the collection is, the Craignish Tales will not be found lacking in picturesque detail, and a careful perusal will reveal many a scene full of the most curious incidents, and it must be confessed to be a typical collection of the tales of days gone by in the wild Western Highlands, where every man was ready with the sword, and handier, if possible, with the dirk. When men struck hastily, and where blood-feuds were fought out with incredible fury and determination. When none or few were brought before a formal court of justice, no matter what the deed committed. There is a lack of exaggeration about them that stamps them with truth. [5]

A Craignish Fence.

The MacEacherns or MacKechnies are said to have been the oldest of all the clans known to local tradition as having at one time or other occupied Craignish. They were regarded as being either a branch or descendants of the MacDonalds of the Isles, and not as an offshoot of the clan Campbell.

---

[5] No mention is made in these tales of wild revenge of fire-arms. They relate, one and all, to a period anterior to the introduction of the same. The combatants despatch each other with the sword, the dirk, and the arrow.

That they were not Campbells appears probable. A sept bearing the surname of MacEachern preceded the undoubted Campbells in Craignish. The former were believed by old Craignish people to have had no original connection with the latter, and, though they lived in the midst of the Campbells, they always retained the surname of MacEachern, and traced their descent from a very different fountain-head. The last survivors of the clan in Craignish died within the last forty years, and therefore within the memory of many who knew them, and who are still living. But, though they have died out of their native place, others of the same old stock are yet living in the islands and districts adjoining Craignish.

The last chief of the MacEacherns had an only child, a daughter, who was given in marriage to Dugall Campbell, a younger son of Campbell of Innisconnell, on Loch Awe. This Dugall was fostered by MacEachern, and it was during his residence at Craignish Castle that he became acquainted with his future wife. She bore him at least one son and one daughter.

The daughter was given by her father, but much against her brother's will, to MacMhàirtinn, or MacMartin, of Fincharn, at the south end of Loch Awe.

A "tocher", or portion, was promised with her, but when it became due at her father's death her brother refused to pay it. This wrong exasperated MacMartin against his brother-in-law, and led to the events which are related in the following traditions.

Dugall's son, or, as he is best known in tradition, "*Mac Dhùghaill Chraiginis,*" resolved to visit his cousin Campbell of Innisconnell, on Loch Awe. He tried to keep his intended visit a secret from all except his wife and a few friends who were to accompany him. But, notwithstanding all his precautions, the secret in some way leaked out, and became known to his twelve faithful retainers, the "gillean maola dubha", the very persons from whom he wished to conceal it.

On the day appointed Campbell set out on his journey, but proceeded not more than a mile's distance from the castle when he looked back, and saw his faithful gillies appearing over a hill and dogging his footsteps. Annoyed at his precautions being defeated, he angrily waved on them to return home. They pretended to yield to his wishes, but only slunk back behind the nearest rising ground which hid them from observation.

There they remained until their master disappeared from their sight, and then resumed their journey, three or four times they came within his view before the bounds of Craignish were crossed, and as often were signalled to return. But, notwithstanding, they held on their way, keeping further to the rear and more out of sight, the oftener they were seen following, and threatened with angry gestures from pursuing their journey.

Campbell saw that the gillies were determined to accompany him at all hazards, and therefore yielded to the inevitable, he took the path through Glen Doan, and having turned thence to the right, struck Loch Awe at Innis Erich, whence he and his companions were ferried over to Innisconnell on the opposite side of the lake.

The visit to Innisconnell having come to an end, he departed for home, taking the path which stretched along the south side of the lake instead of that by which he came. This change of route was rather hazardous, because it led him past Fincharn, where his brother-in-law, McMartin, resided. But being now accompanied, contrary to his first intention, by his trusty gillies, all well armed with sgian-dubh and battle-axe, he had no fear of danger. Arriving at Kilnure, he met McMartin at the church door, by whom he was saluted with profuse expressions of friendship. When these hollow professions were exhausted, McMartin invited his brother-in-law to his house, which stood a short distance from the church, Campbell haughtily replied that he would visit McMartin when the latter would build a castle where he could entertain his friends in a manner becoming their position. McMartin's dignity was hurt by this insulting allusion to the meanness of his abode, still he made an effort to hide his indignation and maintain an outward air of friendship.

When the interview should come to an end, Campbell stretched out his hand to bid his relative farewell. At that moment a new idea suggested itself to the scheming McMartin. "This is a holiday", said he, "and surely you are not going to pass the house of God without entering and waiting till Mass is over." The appeal to Campbell's religious feelings was irresistible, and he instantly turned towards the church with the intention of entering.

As he was in the act of stepping on the threshold, McMartin again interposed, saying, "You must not profane the sanctity of God's house by entering it under arms." The impropriety of his conduct, rather than its prudence, struck Campbell's unsuspecting mind, and therefore he unhesitatingly laid down his arms on the grass outside the church-door, and his less confiding companions reluctantly followed his example.

Campbell then passed into the church and advanced well up to the front of the congregation, but the gillies stood near the door, and kept a watchful eye on every movement of McMartin's men. Their suspicions proved to be only too well founded, as they saw the latter, one by one, steal out of the church, and none of them afterwards returned inside.

A gillie noticing this looked out through the door, and seeing no trace of the arms on the green where they were left, made his way up the body of the church to the place where his master stood, and whispered to him what he had witnessed.

Campbell instantly perceived that treachery was being practised on him and his men, and therefore he hastened out of the church to face it, if possible, in time. But no sooner did he set his foot on the green before the door than he was confronted by McMartin. The latter now threw off his friendly guise, and angrily reproached his brother-in-law with dishonesty in withholding from him his wife's "tocher".

High words and mutual recriminations followed. McMartin's wrath getting the better of him at last, he sprang at his opponent's throat, and was on the point of despatching him with his dagger, when the priest rushed in between them, and succeeded in parting them.

The good man, with much pleading, then prevailed on them to re-enter the church, and there at the altar bound them by solemn oath not to renew the quarrel. But passion in this instance proved stronger than conscience.

The priest detained McMartin in the church and dismissed Campbell. The latter, with his men, made straight for the village of Ford (Àth nan Cràdh), and on arriving there took the bridle-path leading over the hill behind the village on to the Gorge of Kintraw, at the head of Loch Craignish. After ascending the hill just named, Campbell and his men halted for a moment, and, on looking back, saw McMartin with a much larger following of well-armed men breasting the hill in hot pursuit.

The gillies were now armed with dirks only, but they had no longer any thought of flying. A shout was raised, "To the ford, and let us arm ourselves with clubs of alder,"

Forward all rushed to a stream which forms the upper part of Kilmartin river, and there with their dirks cut down stout branches of alder, which they speedily converted into serviceable weapons.

Armed with these weapons they took up their position at the ford, and awaited the attack of McMartin's men. The gillies, it is true, were indifferently armed, but there were other things to compensate for that disadvantage. They themselves were picked men, trained to the use of arms, and no strangers to the fray.

These advantages told in their favour in the end. The McMartins, confident in their greater number and better arms, advanced boldly to the attack, but they were met with courage and determination by their opponents. A furious encounter followed, in which club, and battle-axe, and sgian-dubh were plied with deadly effect. The fight, however, was too hot to last long, and it ended, leaving Campbell and his gillies masters of the field. The McMartins were killed almost to a man, and their dead bodies lay piled in a heap in the water. Among the slain was McMartin himself, who fell pierced by a dirk in mid-stream, and whose fall there is still commemorated in the name of the place, "Àth MhicMhàirtinn", or McMartin's Ford.

The gillies suffered less than their adversaries, but did not come off altogether scatheless.

The living carried the dead bodies of their fallen comrades a good distance nearer Craignish, and buried them in a place a little to the south of the junction of the ford bridle-path with the country road between Craignish and Kilmartin. The spot, which is only a few feet from the road, and on the right-hand side of one travelling southward, was, about thirty-five years ago, marked by a cairn. But some years since the cairn either was broken up and converted into road metal, or used in patching up an adjoining fence (dyke or stone wall). Last time I passed the place only a few stones remained to point out the resting-place of the brave gillies.

Campbell and his men made their way back to Craignish with difficulty, but not with the intention of remaining there long. As soon as he recovered, he gathered his followers together and returned at their head to Fincharn. After mercilessly chastising the poor dependents of McMartin with fire and sword he took his widowed sister and her only child, a boy, back with him to Craignish. He brought up the boy for a time at the castle, but after that sent him to be fostered by a clansman and relative of his own, who lived at Barrackan. This man was one of the companions, not a gillie, of Campbell in his visit to Innisconnell, and the person by whom old McMartin was slain.

His house stood near the lake which lies between the farms of Barrackan and Gartcharran. One day he went down to the lake to wash or dress a hide of home-made leather, and during the operation laid down his dirk beside him on the shore. The little boy, then only seven years old, accompanied his foster-father and noticed the dirk lying where it was left. Taking it up in his hand he began to brandish it, and, as he got excited with his work, made vigorous thrusts with the weapon at an imaginary foe. His foster-father watched him with strange interest, perhaps because he saw in the spirit and bearing of the boy the promise of a future warrior. At last he dropped the hide, and turning to his foster-son said:

"My little fellow, if you were a man what would you do with that dirk?"

"I would drive it into the man who killed my father."

"Perhaps you would, but I will prevent you from doing that", and then having seized the dirk he plunged it into the boy's heart, and threw the body into the lake, which is still called Lochan MhicMhàirtinn, or McMartin's Lake.

The cowardly deed was no sooner over than reflection followed. The murderer then saw that the uncle was bound to revenge his nephew's death. He therefore made up his mind to escape before tidings of his guilt could reach Craignish Castle. And as no time was to be lost, he at once called his family after him and hurried off with them to the shore at "Creag Tharainn", or, as it is now called, "Creagag Chrosgach". There he launched the only boat on the beach, and having placed his family on board, sprang in after them, and then drew out from the land. He was still within hailing distance when Campbell, the dead boy's uncle, appeared. Standing on the shore, he shouted after the fugitive:

"You are the son of good fortune this day" ("Is tusa 'm mac rath an-diugh"). The latter replied with a play on the phrase "Mac Rath", which is similar in sound to Macrae in Gaelic: "Let me be so called in future."

Thereafter he pulled away from the land, and went to the North Highlands, where he settled in the McCrae country, and assumed the surname of McCrae. His descendants lived there to a comparatively recent time, but altered this tradition and reversed the main facts. Of the two versions that of Craignish is far the *more probable*.

Raghnall Òg Chraiginis (Young Ranald of Craignish).

Young Ranald of Craignish was sent by his father to "Àirigh Sgeòdinnis", the district between Kilmartin River (Sgeòdag) and Loch Craignish, to be fostered by McIsaac of Largie (Learga MhicÌosaig). McIsaac was noted for his strength and bravery, and also for his expertness in military exercises, as they were then known. These manly and soldierly qualities recommended him to Campbell of Craignish as a suitable person to be entrusted with the fostering of his son Ranald.

When Ranald's period of fosterage was completed he left Largie, accompanied by his eight foster-brothers (co-dhaltan), the sons of old McIsaac. They took the road to Ormaig, on the south side of Loch Craignish, and thence turned to the right with the intention of following the path which leads round the loch into Craignish. They had not proceeded far when they entered the wood of Ormaig, which was then infested by a notorious freebooter and his companions. This worthy was nicknamed "Am Marsanta Fada", or Long Merchant, *fada*, from his length of limb and tallness of stature, and *marsanta*, from his habit of occasionally sallying forth from the wood disguised as a travelling packman, and thus visiting the surrounding country for such information regarding the movements of the inhabitants as he could turn to his own account. On one of these visits he ascertained the time of Ranald's return home, and the route which he intended to take, at once he resolved to waylay the latter and make him prisoner, with the intention of extorting a heavy ransom for his release.

Hastily returning to the wood, he took up a convenient position for carrying out his scheme, and there awaited the approach of his intended victim. When the moment for action arrived, he and his men sprang from' their hiding-places and rushed with wild impetuosity on the brave McIsaacs. The latter had barely time to form a circle round their foster-brother when the outlaws were down upon them.

A desperate encounter then followed, from which none of the combatants on either side escaped unhurt. The "Long Merchant" and his band were slain to a man, and one-half of the McIsaacs lay dead on the field. The other half, with young Ranald, were more or less severely wounded, only one of them all, "Calum Mòr", was in a condition to return to Largie. This poor fellow left the field wounded and bleeding, and with great difficulty succeeded in reaching his father's home. Old McIsaac, then blind and bed-ridden, recognising his son's voice, said:

"Have you come, my son?"

"Yes, father, I have come," was the reply.

"Where did you leave your foster-brother and your brothers?"

"I left them on the battle-field."

"Come here, my son, and kiss me, seeing that you have returned to me in life."

The latter, suspecting no evil, moved towards his father's bed, but his mother, who watched her husband, suddenly cried, "Fly, fly! he has the dirk (biodag) in his hand." The son stepped back immediately, but not a moment too soon. The old man, following the sound of his son's retreating footsteps, darted his dirk after him, accompanying the action with the remark, "You are not a son like your father, else you would not have been here while your foster-brother and brothers lie dead on the field" ("Cha mhac thu mar an t-athair air neo cha bhiodh tusa an seo, agus do cho-dhalta agus do bhràithrean nan laighe anns an àraich").

The dirk, fortunately, missed the mark, explanations followed, and the old man's indignation was appeased. Men were immediately sent with a sled (càrn) to bring the wounded home.

When young Ranald recovered, he returned to Craignish, and, in gratitude to the McIsaacs for their fidelity, his father gave Calum Mòr McIsaac, already mentioned, a farm on the Craignish lands. The name of the farm has been forgotten, but there is a bay on the farm of Daill still known as Camas MhicÌosaig, or McIsaac's Bay.

There is also a reference made in Skene's *Celtic Scotland*, vol. iii, p. 32, to a Malcolme Moir Makesaig, who, in 1592, gave his bond of manrent to his well-beloved Ronald Campbell of Barrichbyan in Craignish. This Malcolm Mòr may, however, have been a descendant of the Calum Mòr of the foregoing: tradition.

Baintighearna Bhàn Chraiginis (The Fair-haired Lady of Craignish).

This lady was the sister of Campbell of Innisconnell. She was married thrice, bore children to each of her husbands, and outlived them all. Her first husband was Campbell of Craignish, after his death she married MacDougall of Dunolly, who was then a widower, and the father of a family by his first wife.

Her step-sons wanted to get hold of certain title-deeds in her possession, to which, perhaps, they thought they had some right, but she fled with the precious deeds across the String of Lorne and placed them in safe custody with her brother at Innisconnell. The story of her flight is pretty well known, and need not be repeated here.

Dunolly, her second husband, having died, she again entered the bonds of wedlock with her former tutor, MacIvor of Lergychony, in the north end of Craignish. At last the fair-haired lady herself paid the last debt of nature, and must needs be burled. But where, and by whom?

The Campbells were determined to carry her remains to Kilvorie, near Craignish Castle, and lay them there beside those of her first husband. The McDougalls were as firmly resolved to convey them to Lorne, and deposit them in the old family vault in Kilbride. But the McIvors, being too weak to back up with force their claims to the dangerous honour, put forward none at all, and wisely remained neutral. On the day appointed for the burial the Campbells hurried up from the lower end of Craignish, and were first to arrive at Lergychony. With as little delay as possible they got the coffin ready and prepared to depart with it before the McDougalls should appear. But just as they were on the point of leaving the latter unfortunately arrived.

A quarrel then seemed inevitable, but the Campbells contrived to put it off for a time. They prevailed on the McDougalls to retire to an adjoining barn to partake of some refreshments after their long journey, and then they stole away with the coffin as fast as their legs could carry them. When the McDougalls reappeared and saw how they were deceived their indignation was boundless. Their first thoughts were of pursuit, but a little consideration convinced them of the folly of that course, as they were less than thirty in number, and as the Campbells could not be overtaken until they were in the centre of Craignish, and in the midst of their friends. Something, however, had to be done in revenge for the deception practised upon them, and to save them from the contempt of their clansmen in Lorne.

They flew therefore to the nearest lands occupied by the dependents of Campbell of Craignish and harried them of their cattle. These they drove before them across Sliabh an Tuim, the range of hills between Craignish and Melfort, and halted not until they reached Loch nan Druimnean.

Meantime a messenger was despatched with the utmost haste to inform the funeral party of what had happened. The latter were overtaken about three miles beyond Lergychony, at the farm of Soraba, where there was an old, and it would seem even then, deserted burying-place. There, and not at Kilvorie or Kilbride, the fair-haired lady's remains were hastily laid in their last resting-place. The burying-place was, in my boyhood, used as a stack-yard, and there I often stood on what was known as the grave of Baintighearna Bhàn Chraiginis. The grave was no sooner closed than the Campbells, having already mustered in great force, went in pursuit of the McDougalls. They overtook the latter at Loch nan Druimnean, and fell upon them as they were amusing themselves putting the stone, after having first feasted on the spoil they had taken. The McDougalls fought bravely, but were overpowered by numbers, and most of them, including a son of the fair-haired lady, were slain.

McIvor's Revenge.

Time passed, but not the remembrance of the slaughter of the McDougalls at Loch nan Druimnean.

Young MacIvor of Lergychony, another son of the fair lady, never forgot that his half-brother, McDougall, was among the slain, and that his death remained unavenged on the slayer. This man, a weaver, happened to be in the neighbouring farm of Garbh-Shròin. MacIvor often left his own house with the intention of killing the weaver, but as often was sent back and disarmed of his fell purpose by the kind and ready-witted object of his wrath.

At last, a false sense of honour prevailing over his humanity, he went to Garbh-Shròin firmly resolved to fasten a quarrel on the poor weaver and take his life on some pretext or other. With this cruel intention he entered the house of the weaver, whom he found sitting at the loom, and weaving a web for diced hose.

"Cut me", said he, "a pair of hose off that web."

"I'll do that with pleasure," was the generous reply.

Then the weaver took up his knife and began to cut *between* the dice.

"Not there, but here," interrupted MacIvor, placing his finger *on* the dice.

"No", remonstrated the weaver, "I'll cut on either side of the dice, but not there."

"Wretch, I have borne with you long enough in a weightier matter than this, but I will bear with you no longer."

Then he drew his sword and struck off the weaver's head in revenge for his brother's death, and to satisfy his own sense of honour.

MacFhlaithbheartaich na h-Àirde (McLarty of Aird).

This man lived on the farm of Aird in Craignish. His house overlooked the bay on the right-hand side of Loch Beg. He was a brave man and a famous archer. He followed Campbell of Craignish, by whom he was regarded as one of his most trusty dependents. Once in his time Craignish was left in a defenceless state in consequence of his absence and that of his acknowledged chief on some important expedition.

McKay, or McGhee, of the Rhinns in Islay (Mac Aoidh na Ranna), having heard of this, launched his galley and made for Craignish, with the intention of burning the houses and harrying the lands of Aird and the neighbourhood.

He and his men arrived at their destination in the night, and landed on a rock still known as "Sgeir nan Ìleach", or the Islaymen's Rock, at the west point of the bay already mentioned.

That same night another person arrived at Aird quite as unexpectedly as the McGhee. This was McLarty. His family hastened to celebrate the event with a substantial, if somewhat primitive, evening meal A wether was hastily killed, cut up, and placed in a large pot of water over the fire. McLarty then took a seat at the fire and began to relate his adventures to his family and friends. While he was thus engaged, a shoulder of mutton sprang out of the pot on to the floor. "Put it in the pot again," said McLarty. The order was at once obeyed, a second time the shoulder bounded on to the hearth. It was once more returned to the pot. But when it leaped out a third time the whole incident, simple enough in itself, was regarded as an omen of serious import.

McLarty divined its meaning, and at once acted on the supposed warning. He rose from his seat, and having taken down his bow and quiver from the wall, from which they were suspended, walked out into the darkness. He then looked in every direction, but saw nothing to alarm him. Still dissatisfied, he left the neighbourhood of the house, and made a wide circuit to the western point of the bay, where he concealed himself in a "leab' fholaich" (hiding-bed) among the rocks. From this spot he surveyed first the mouth of the loch, then the bay, and, last of all, the Islaymen's Rock, just under him. There he saw a galley moored, but abandoned by its crew. Suspecting that the crew landed with no friendly intention, he started to his feet and anxiously looked back towards his own house. What he then witnessed amply confirmed his worst suspicions. Several torches were being applied to the eaves of his house, and the thatch was beginning to take fire. Without a moment's delay he set off, and ran with full speed until he was within bow-shot of his dwelling. Halting there, he took an arrow and launched it with unerring aim at one of the moving objects under the eaves of his house, a torch fell and with it the holder. He took a second arrow and sent it on its way with the same deadly effect. A third and a fourth followed in rapid succession. It was enough, the invaders were alarmed, the cry was raised, "McLarty is come, let us fly to the shore."

Panic-stricken, the band rushed to the galley, McLarty pursued them, sending arrow after arrow into their midst. At last he got back to his old "hiding-bed", but by the time he arrived there the surviving fugitives were all on board, save one man. This man was in the act of springing into the boat, when the last arrow from McLarty's quiver overtook him, and pinned his hand to the gunwale. The crew perceiving this, shouted, as if with one voice, "Slàn fallain, 'MhicAoidh! Slàn fallain, 'MicAoidh!" ("Whole and sound, McGhee! whole and sound, McGhee!")

The prayer, or charm, whichever it was, was of little avail. McGhee's son (for it was he) died long before the galley touched the shore of the Rhinns. But the fatal arrow was kept by the father, and hung up in a conspicuous place in his house. There it must be left for the present.

McLarty's services were appreciated by Campbell of Craignish, who rewarded him with the farm of "Baile Tarsainn", so called because it extended across (tarsainn) the whole breadth of Craignish. The farm, at a later period, was divided into two farms, Achinarnoch and Gartcharran, and thenceforth the old name was disused, and at length forgotten.

When McLarty took possession of the farm, he formed a plan of cultivating some improvable, but waste lands in Achinarnoch. But as a "seisreach", or team of six horses, was required to draw the plough, and as Islay was famous for its breed of horses, he manned a large galley (bìrlinn) belonging to Campbell of Craignish, and sailed with it to the Rhinns. Landing there, he was told that McGhee kept a good stud of horses, and that he would be glad to dispose of some of them at a fair price.

Without a moment's hesitation, he called on McGhee, by whom he was invited to the house and hospitably entertained. While both sat haggling over the price of the animals, McLarty's attention was arrested by a blood-stained arrow suspended from a nail opposite him. He could not resist the temptation of taking it down and examining it. Then turning towards McGhee, he said: "That is a good arrow."

"It is", replied McGhee, "and if you will tell me whose hand sped it (cò an làmh a chuir i), I will give you the best 'seisreach' in Islay."

"It will not cost you more," answered McLarty.

The bargain was at once concluded. In due time the horses were placed on board the galley. The crew sat at their oars awaiting the signal to start, and McLarty stood with one foot on the gunwale and the other on the rock, which answered the purpose of a pier.

Turning now towards McGhee, who stood on the rock, he said, "Reach me your hand." The thing was done, then bringing his own right-hand down with a vigorous blow on to McGhee's, he added, "There is the hand that sped the arrow." Next moment he was on board and the galley in motion.

McGhee and his men stood for a short time gazing in blank astonishment at the receding galley, but having at length recovered from their surprise, they flew to the beach to launch their boats and give chase. Meantime messengers were despatched inland to summon others to their assistance, but by the time assistance arrived, and the boats were manned and ready for sea, the galley had made such headway that further pursuit became hopeless.

The galley arrived safely at Aird. McLarty, however, suspected that the McGhees would follow, and attempt to take him at night by surprise. He therefore went down to Aird Point, opposite "Doras Mòr", and thence kept a sharp outlook down the Sound of Jura. When evening approached, he saw a galley coming up the sound with the flowing tide, and making straight for the Doras. Arriving there, it turned in to one of the creeks at the point. McLarty allowed it to touch the shore, where it got grounded, and then from his "hiding-bed" sent arrow after arrow flying into the midst of the crew, until none of them were left alive.

After this he removed from Aird to his own farm of "Baile Tarsainn", where he passed the remainder of his life. His descendants held the farm down to the beginning of the last century. The only traces left of their connection with it are to be found in the names of an island and a rock opposite Gartcharran, the former being still called "Eilean MhicFhlaithbheartaich", or

McLarty's Island, and the latter "Sgeir Dhubh MhicFhlaithbheartaich", or McLarty's Black Rock.

Glengarrisdale.

Some centuries ago Glengarrisdale, at the back of Jura, belonged to the McLeans of Loch Buy. While they were in possession of Glengarrisdale, hostilities broke out between them and the Campbells, which were maintained by mutual acts of retaliation of the most heartless nature.

Craignish, as the nearest and most exposed part of the Campbell country, suffered greatly from the fury of the McLeans. This naturally so exasperated the Craignish people that they longed for an opportunity of being revenged on their enemies.

An opportunity at last occurred, and they hastened to take advantage of it. Hearing that the Castle of Glengarrisdale was weakly garrisoned, they took to their boats, and, having crossed the Sound of Jura, landed at Cnoc an t-Sabhail. Hence they travelled over the hills until they came in sight of the stronghold of the McLeans, who were at that moment amusing themselves putting the stone, while their arms stood against a large boulder, which is still called "Clach nan Arm", or lay near a spring which is known as "Tobar nan arm". The Campbells observing this, crept forward until they got between the McLeans and their weapons, and then falling on their defenceless foemen, slew them all except one man, whose name was McPhie.

This brave fellow sprang into the sea, and having swum round a point called Rubha Mhic a' Phì (McPhie's Point), landed in a cave known as "Uaimh Mhic a' Phì" (McPhie's Cave), where he hid himself. Next day a galley (bìrlinn) arrived from Mull, and the crew being signalled by McPhie, and told what had happened, returned to Mull for reinforcements. With these they hastened back to Glengarrisdale, but on arriving ascertained that the Campbells had left, and that they were on their way to Cnoc an t-Sabhail. Losing as little time as possible, they set off in pursuit of the latter, and getting before them, took up their position at the foot of a steep slope known as "Creachan Dubha".

When the Campbells came to the top of the slope and saw a superior force of the McLeans at the foot, they resolved, like brave men, to give battle and sell their lives as dearly as possible. With a shout, they descended to the attack, but, on coming within striking distance, they found that they were placed at a serious disadvantage, while they could not reach with their arms even the heads of their opponents, their feet and legs were hewn off by the latter with their battle-axes, and none of the Craignish men escaped alive to carry home the sad tidings of the slaughter of their comrades.

The cairns beneath which the bodies of the McLeans were buried are yet to be seen at Glengarrisdale, and in a crevice of a rock near the scene of the massacre is the skull of a McLean, with the marks of two cuts and the crown sliced off.

A Barbreck-Craignish Tradition.
Càrn Dòmhnaill, or Donald s Cairn.

Bealach Mòr, or the Great Gap, is better known to the English-speaking public as the Pass of Kintraw. Through this gap winds the road between Craignish and Kilmartin. Immediately before entering it the traveller from Craignish may observe an old path, once the road between the two parishes, ascending the steep green hill on his right hand. Less than thirty yards up this path there is a narrow and somewhat deep cut, where two young travellers met in clear daylight between two and three centuries ago. One of the two was Donald Campbell, son of the Laird of Barbreck-Craignish, and the other McLachlane, son of the Laird of Achaghearrain, in the parish of Kilmichael-Glassary.

Neither of them would make way for the other. From jostling they passed to wrestling. McLachlane, finding himself overmatched, drew his dirk, and with it stabbed his opponent. This put a sudden stop to the quarrel. Campbell succeeded with difficulty in descending to the foot of the hill, but when he reached the plain beneath he fell down on the greensward in a dying state.

Bad news travels rapidly, and the saying proved true enough in this instance. Before evening word came to the Laird of Barbreck informing him of his son's death, and as soon as he heard it he resolved to go to Achaghearrain with his men, and take, in satisfaction for the blood shed, that of young McLachlane. But the question then occurred to him which would be the most suitable hour of leaving Barbreck and setting out on his journey of revenge. If he arrived at Achaghearrain early in the night, McLachlane might still be hiding in some safe retreat outside his father's house. If he delayed till next morning, McLachlane would probably be on his way to the south, and beyond the reach of danger. He therefore made up his mind to start at midday, in the hope of reaching his destination at early dawn. Meantime he went to bed to snatch a few hours' sleep, but, before doing so, he gave strict orders to MacGilleFhaolain Dubh (black-haired or swarthy McLellan), his faithful servant and foster-brother of the deceased Donald, to awaken him before the hour appointed. McLellan promised obedience, and then, wrapped in his plaid, laid himself down on the floor beside his master's bed.

But though he laid himself down he did not sleep. His thoughts naturally turned to his master's intended expedition and its probable consequences. It occurred to him that, if it were carried out, more than young McLachlane's blood might be spilt before the work of retribution was accomplished, there was an unpleasant but not unlikely danger, and therefore he began to consider how the danger might be avoided.

After pondering over the matter for a time he resolved to take the cruel business into his own hands and carry it out unassisted.

His plan being thus formed, he waited where he was until his master fell asleep, and then rising quietly from the floor and stealing out of the room, he set off at a smart pace across the hills to Achaghearrain. Arriving there before daybreak, he posted himself with his back against the wall of McLachlane's house, and within a short distance of the door, awaiting the exit of his intended victim. When the first signs of returning day appeared, he heard someone stirring within, and moving towards the door, concluding that this was McLachlane preparing to depart before his pursuers should arrive on the scene, he grasped his sword firmly in his hands, and stood like a wild beast prepared to pounce on its prey.

McLachlane, for it proved to be none else, cautiously opened the door, and then stooping beneath the lintel, stood in the doorway with his head thrust out beyond the side walls. Next moment his head, severed from the neck by one stroke of McLellan's sword, bounded on to the door-step. McLellan quickly snatched up the head, and flew with it as fast as ever he could back to Barbreck. On arriving there he entered his master's bedroom as noiselessly as he left it, and stretched himself once more in his former position on the floor, where he soon fell asleep. When Barbreck awoke and saw the light shining brightly into his room, he sprang from his bed in a wild fit of passion, and demanded of the startled McLellan why he disobeyed his orders.

"Laird of Barbreck", coolly replied the latter, "I was sorry to disturb your sleep", and then, unwrapping his plaid, and allowing the head to roll out on the floor, added, "There is McLachlane's head for you."

MAR A FHUAIR MÌCHEAL SCOT FIOS NA H-INID ÀS AN RÒIMHE AGUS A CHUIR E CRÌOCH AIR A BHITH A' DOL AN SIN GA SIREADH

"An Inid bheadaidh thar gach fèill
Is olc an aimsir duine ghionaich 'thig na dèidh."

[Theirear an "Inid Bheadaidh", nuair a tha a' ghealach ùr beagan làithean an dèidh na Fèille Brìde. Air dha seo a bhith, thigeadh, mar a theireadh na seann daoine, "Earrach fad à tòin Càisge".]

An uair a bha an dùthaich fo riaghladh a' Phàpa, bha an sluagh ro aineolach agus chan fhaoidteadh nì air bith a dhèanamh no a ràdh leò, gus am faigheadh iad comas a' Phàpa. B' i an Inid a bha a' riaghladh na h-uile fèill a bha ga leanachd fad na bliadhna. Mar seo, nuair a bhiodh fios air Là na h-Inid, bha fhios air latha-aimsir gach fèill fad na bliadhna. Air Là na h-Inid, bha an Carbhas a' tòiseachadh, sia seachdainean an dèidh sin bha La Càisge, agus mar sin a-sìos gu ruig ceann na bliadhna.

Bha duine a' dol às gach dùthaich a h-uile bliadhna a dh'iarraidh fios na h-Inid don Ròimh, agus an uair a thigeadh e dhachaigh agus a dh'innseadh e cò b' e Là na h-Inid air a' bhliadhna sin. Bha duine ceannsgalach tapaidh curanta, seòlt' agus deagh bheusach air ainmeachadh gu dol don Ròimh, ga sireadh an athbhliadhna.

Bha Mìcheal Scot, duine foghlaimte ainmeil ra latha, air a shònrachadh gu dol don Ròimh a dh'fhaotainn fios na h-Inid, bliadhna de na bliadhnachan, ach am measg na h-uile gnothach eile a bha aige ra dhèanamh, dhìochuimhnich e a dhleasnas gus an robh fèistean na bliadhna thairis aig Aifreann na Coinnle. Cha robh mionaid ra chall. Thog e air a dh'ionnsaigh tè de na loithean-marcaich is thubhairt e rithe, "Cia cho luath 's tha thusa?" "Tha mi cho luath ris a' ghaoith," ars ise. "Cha dèan thu 'n gnothach," arsa Mìcheal. Ràinig e an dara tè "Cia cho luath 's 'tha thusa?" "Tha mi cho luath 's gum fàg mi a' ghaoth 'tha 'm dhèidh, 's gum beir mi air a' ghaoith 'tha romham," ars' ise. "Cha dèan thusa 'n gnothach," fhreagair Mìcheal. Bha an treas tè cho luath ri gaoth dubh a' Mhàirt – "Is gann gun dèan thus' an gnothach," arsa

Mìcheal. Ràinig e an ceathramh tè, 's chuir e a' cheist rithe. "Tha mi cho luath ri aigne maighdinn eadar a dà leannan." "Nì thusa feum," arsa Mìcheal, "dèan deas." "Tha mis' a ghnàth ullamh nam biodh an duine dom rèir," deir ise.

Dh'fhalbh iad, agus bu cho-ionnan muir is tìr dhaibh. Nuair a bha iad air a' mhuir thuirt a' ghlaistig ris, "Ciod a their mnathan ann an Albainn, nuair tha iad a' smàladh an teine." "Marcaich thusa," arsa Mìcheal, "ann an ainm do mhaighstir, agus coma leat sin." "Beannachd dhut fhèin ach mollachd aig d' oid'-ionnsachaidh," fhreagair i. "Ciod," ars ise a-rithist, "a their na mnathan an uair tha iad a' cur a' chiad aisearan a laighe agus an dara cìocharan nan uchd?" "Marcaich thus' an ainm do mhaighstir, agus leig le mnathan Alba cadal," deir Mìcheal. "Bu lonach an tè 'chuir a' chiad chorrag ad bheul," ars ise.

Ràinig Mìcheal an Ròimh, b' i a' mhadainn a bh' ann, chuir e grad-fhios a dh'ionnsaigh a' Phàpa gun robh teachdaire na h-Alba aig an doras ag iarraidh fios na h-Inid le cabhaig, mun rachadh an Carbhas air chall. Thàinig am Pàpa gun dàil don àit'-èisteachd. "Cia às tha thusa?" deir e ri Mìcheal. "Tha mise o do chloinn dhìlis ann an Albainn, ag iarraidh fios na h-Inid, mun tèid an Carbhas air chall," deir Mìcheal. "Bha thu ro fhada gun tighinn." "Is tràth a dh'fhàg sin mi," fhreagair Mìcheal. "Is math àrd a mharcaich thu." "Cha b' àrd 's cha b' ìosal ach dìreach romham," deir Mìcheal. "Chì mi," deir am Pàpa, "sneachd air do bhonaid." "Tha, ler cead, sneachda na h-Alba." "Ciod," ars am Pàpa, "an comharradh 'bheir thu dhòmhsa air sin, agus gu bheil thu air tighinn à Albainn a dh'iarraidh fios na h-Inid?" "Tha," arsa Mìcheal, "gu bheil bròg air do chois nach buin dhut fhèin." Thug am Pàpa sùil agus bha bròg boireannaich air a chois dheis. "Gheibh thu na tha 'dhìth ort," deir e ri Mìcheal, "agus bidh falbh. Is e a' chiad Dimàirt den chiad solas earraich Là na h-Inid."

Mar seo fhuair Mìcheal Scot fios air an dìomhaireachd a bha am Pàpa a' cumail dha fhèin. Roimhe seo, cha d' fhuair an teachdaire ach gum b' e a leithid seo no a leithid siud de latha, latha na h-Inid air a' bhliadhna sin, ach fhuair Mìcheal fios air mar a bha am Pàpa fhèin a' faotainn a-mach an latha. Ciamar a phill Mìcheal chan eil eachdraidh ag innseadh.[6]

---

[6] Note.– A parallel to Michael Scott resorting to the help of supernatural beings, and rejecting those whom he finds too slow for his purpose, is furnished by an incident in the story of the great German magician, Dr. Faust. The second edition (1589) of the *Volksbuch* relates how Faust, being in Erfurt, called up three spirits – the first was swift as the arrow, the second as the wind, the third as the thought of man. From the *Volksbuch*, the incident went into the different versions of the marionette-play, mainly based on a translation of Marlowe's *Faustus*, which was popular throughout Germany. Lessing took the idea of his Faust fragment, as Goethe did later, from seeing one of these plays, and borrowed the incident, which he considerably amplified. There are seven spirits, and the favoured one is swift as the transition from good to evil. Some of the versions of the marionette-play, noted since the publication of Lessing's *Faust* fragment, have evidently been partly influenced by the latter. With the Highland test of swiftness may be compared "Finn's Questions", Nos. 5 and 6 (*infra*, p. 54) – "What is swifter than the wind? – The mind of a woman. What is sharper than a sword? – A woman's wit between two men." It would be interesting to know if any other traces of contact could be established between the legends of the great Scotch and German magicians.

ALFRED NUTT

How Michael Scot obtained knowledge of Shrove-tide from Rome

AND HOW HE CAUSED THE GOING THERE FOR THE PURPOSE OF ASCERTAINING THE KNOWLEDGE TO CEASE.

"The early Shrove-tide, over all feasts,
Hard times for a glutton come after it."

[Shrove-tide is said to be "beadaidh", or early, when it happens that the new moon occurs a few days after Candlemas. Then, as of old they used to phrase it, "There's a long tail of Spring after Easter".]

When the country of Scotland was ruled by the Pope, the inhabitants were very ignorant, and nothing could be done or said by them until they would obtain the consent of the Pope. The Feast of Shrovetide regulated all the feasts that followed it, during the whole year. So, when the date of Shrove-tide would be known, the date of every feast during the year was known. On Shrove-tide, Lent began, six weeks after that was Easter, and so on unto the end of the year.

A man left each country every year for Rome for the purpose of ascertaining the knowledge of the date of Shrove-tide, and on his arrival home, and on his telling- the date of Shrove-tide in that year, an intelligent, clever, fearless, prudent, and well-bred man was selected to proceed to Rome on the following year to ascertain it.

On a certain year, Michael Scot, a learned man and famous, was chosen to proceed to Rome to obtain the knowledge of Shrove-tide, but, because of the many other matters he had to attend to, he forgot his duty until all the feasts of the year were over at Candlemas. There was not a minute to lose. He betook himself to one of the fairy riding-fillies, and said to her, "How swift are you?" "I am as fleet as the wind," replied she. "You will not do," says Michael. He reached the second one. "How swift are you?" "I am as swift as that I can out-speed the wind that comes behind me, and overtake the wind that goes before me." "You will not do," answered Michael. The third one was as fleet as the "black blast of March". "Scarcely will you do," says Michael. He arrived at the fourth one, and put his question to her. "I am as swift as the thought of a maiden between her two lovers." "You will be of service," says Michael, "make ready." "I am always ready if the man were in accord with me," says she.

They started. Sea and land were alike to them. While they were above the sea, the witch said to him, "What say the women of Scotland when they quench the fire?" "You ride," says Michael, "in your master's name, and never mind that." "Blessing to thyself, but a curse on thy teacher," replied she. "What," says she again, "say the wives of Scotland when they put the first weanling to bed, and a suckling at their breast?" "Ride you in your master's name, and let the wives of Scotland sleep," responded Michael. "Forward was the woman who put the first finger in your mouth," says she.

Michael arrived at Rome. It was the morning. He sent swift message to the Pope that the messenger from Scotland was at the door seeking knowledge of Shrove-tide, lest Lent would go away. The Pope came at once to the audience-room. "Whence art thou?" he said to Michael. "I am from thy faithful children of Scotland, seeking the knowledge of Shrove-tide, lest Lent will go away," says Michael. "You were too late in coming." "Early that leases me," replied Michael. "You have ridden somewhat high." "Neither high nor low, but right ahead," says Michael. "I see," says the Pope, "snow on your bonnet." "Yes, by your leave, the snow of Scotland." "What proof," says the Pope, "can you give me of that? likewise, that you have come from Scotland to seek knowledge of Shrove-tide?" "That," says Michael, "a shoe is on your foot that is not your own." The Pope looked, and on his right foot was a woman's shoe. "You will get what you want," says he to Michael, "and begone. The first Tuesday of the first moon of Spring is Shrove-tide."

Thus Michael Scot obtained knowledge of the secret that the Pope kept to himself. Before that time the messenger obtained but the knowledge that this day or that day was the day of Shrove-tide in the coming year, but Michael obtained knowledge of how the Pope himself came to ascertain the day. How Michael returned, history does not tell.

The Good Housewife and Her Night Labours

This story is mentioned by the late Mr. Campbell of Islay, under the name of *Dùn Bhuilg*, as one current throughout the whole of the Western Highlands and Islands. The present version is given, as it illustrates the leading features of the whole fairy-belief, such, for instance, as the admonition of the sage adviser to the housewife not to ask for assistance which was not permissible to mortals, and the Gaelic proverb, that a person should not ask for what he may have to regret – "*Cha bu chòir do dhuine guidhe airson an nì a chaoineadh e.*"

The name Inary may be derived from or connected with the Gaelic word *iongnadh*, wonder, to denote the astonishment excited in herself by the unexpected and sudden answer to her wish in the appearance of her supernatural visitors.[7]

The more common form of the name of the Fairy Hill is the softer *Dùn Bhuilg.*

The present version of the tale was heard in Tiree, and is localised as having taken place in Burg Hill, a place of that name being on the opposite coast in Mull, but every place has its own local designation, as every place had its own fairy hillock, sithean or brugh, as Fairy Hillock of Night-quarters, *Sìthean nan Codaichean-oidhche*, in Ardnamurchan, the Fairy Hillock of Supper, or Sowens, *Sìthean na Càbhraich*, in Loch Awe, the Fairy Hill of Hosts, *Sìthean Sluaigh*, in Strachur, the Cup-shaped Fairy Hill, *Dùn Cuaich*, Inverary, etc., etc.

The rational explanation of the story is that the over-sensitive, anxious, over-worked good wife fell asleep, and her dream took the form of the incidents that are here mentioned. The uproar was probably caused by the confusion and weariness of her own mind, or the hum of the kettle, or any passing sound, and the soundness

---

[7] Editor's note (2022): *Inary/Innaraidh* is properly spelled *ionnairidh* and actually means 'night watch'

of her husband's sleep was naturally enough shaken off by the water being dashed at him, and further by the admission of fresh air when the door was opened. There is also a view held by some, that there were at one time a race of people acquainted with the art of preparing and fulling cloth (*calanas*), who lived in remote and secret places, only appearing when invoked, and were fond of being associated in work known to them, with races still surviving. Tradition makes mention of a race of people that lived on what they could gather on the shore (*siubhal na tràghad*), and who knew how to extract dyes from shell-fish, as also from the roots of plants.

A' Bhean-taighe Mhath 's Obair-oidhche.

Aon uair o chiana nan cian, bha bean fear-fearainn no tuathanach beartach san oidhche, mar a b' àbhaist do mhnathan cùramach san àm, an dèighinn do dh'fhear an taighe 's don teaghlach a' gabhail gu thàmh, a' dèanamh clò air an son. Air dhi a bhith sgìth agus ro chlaoidhte leis an obair thuirt i:

"Ò nach tigeadh o thalamh no o chuan, o chian no o làimh aon neach a chuidicheadh mise 'dhèanamh a' chlò seo."

Cha luaithe a bhruidhinn i na chuala i bualadh san doras 's guth ag èigheach ann an cainnt choimhich a thuig i a bha a' ciallachadh:

"Ionnairidh mhòr mhath, bhean an taighe. Fosgail an doras dhomh 's cho fad 's a mhaireas dhòmhsa, gheibh thusa."

Dh'èirich i 's nar a dh'fhosgail i an doras, thàinig bean choimheach ann an deise ciar-uaine a-staigh seachad oirre 's shuidh i aig a' chuibheall-shnìomh. Cha bu luatha a rinn i sin na thàinig buille na bu chruaidhe don doras 's èigheach sna ceart fhacail:

"Ionnairidh mhòr mhaith, bhean an taighe. Fosgail an doras 's cho fad 's a mhaireas dhòmhsa, gheibh thusa."

Nar fhreagair bean an taighe, thàinig tè eile neo-shaoghalta a-staigh 's ghabh i thun na cuigeil. Sin thàinig buille mòran na bu chruaidhe 's guth na b' àirde ag iarraidh a-staigh 's a' tairgsinn cuideachaidh. Nar dh'fhosgladh an doras, thàinig ban-choigreach eile a-staigh 's shuidh i a chàrdadh. Buileach thòisich ise air obair, thàinig bualadh na b' doirbhe don doras 's guth a' glaodhaich:

"Ionnairidh mhòr mhaith, bhean an taighe. Fosgail an doras gu luath 's cho fad 's a mhaireas dhòmhsa gheibh thusa."

Nar chaidh an doras fhosgladh, shnàmh tè iongantach eile, na deise, 's na coltas mar a bha càch, a-staigh, 's dar a fhuair i àite-suidhe, thòisich i air cìreadh clòimhe. Sin thàinig an ath-tè le barrachd stairirich 's nar fhuair i a-staigh, thòisich i air tlamadh. Bha iad a-nis a' tighinn na bu chaise 's na bu luaithe aon às dèidhinn aoin le faram 's gleadhraich na bu mhotha 's na b' àirde gus an robh an taigh loma làn dhiubh 's iad uile an grèim. Thòisich an sin an obair da-rìreadh, cìreadh, càrdadh, tarraing tlamadh, cuigealadh, shnìomh a' bheart-fhighe gu luath luath, 's am bùrn-luaidh mun teine, 's chluinnte srannail na cuibhle, spreagail nan càrd, dìosgail na cuigealach 's sùrd na beart-fhighe cian air astar. Dh'fheuch bean an taighe mhaith, mar a b' fheàrr a b' urrainn dhi ri tàmh a chur air an ùpraid 's pailteas bithidh a chumail riutha gus am faicear 's an cluinnteadh am fallas a' tuiteam bho h-aodann le slad air an ùrlar. Ach cha chumadh an domhan biadh riutha, mar b' fhaide san oidhche a thàinig e, 's ann bu mhotha a dh'iarradh iad, 's cha bu mhotha an obair na na dh'fheumadh iad. Aig a a' mheadhan-oidhche bha a' bhean-taighe chòir thun tuiteam le saothair obair. Dh'fheuch i sin ri fear an taighe a dhùsgadh ach cha b' urrainn dhi. Bha e cho maith feuchainn ri clach-mhuilinn a charachadh, cha ghluaiseadh 's cha bhruidhneadh e, ged a chàireadh 's a ghlaodhadh i fhathast ris. Nar dh'fhairtlich e oirre 's nach robh fhios aice dè dhèanamh i, smaointich i dol airson comhairle gu seann duine glic air a' bhaile. Dh'fhàg i a' chuideachd neo-thlachdmhor aig a' chuid mo dheireadh den deasacha' a rinn i dhaibh, shlip i a-mach 's ràinig i an duine glic 's dh'innis i dha an dragh a bh' oirre 's mar nach dùisgeadh fear an taighe. Thug esan achmhasan dhi airson a cion-mhothachaidh ann a bhith ag iarraidh cuideachaidh neo-shaoghalta, 's thuirt e rithe:

"Cho fad 's as beò thu, na cuir romhad, na iarr 's na guidh airson nì mì-dhealbhach no mì-chiatach, eagal 's gum faigh thu t-òrdugh 's gun toir thu sgiorram ort fhèin. Thàinig na daoine 's cha chuir saothair bruidhne air falbh iad. Tha fear an taighe fo gheasaibh 's mun dùisg e, feumaidh a' mhuinntir neo-cheadaichte a ghuidh thu fhèin air an son, an taigh fhàgail 's beagan den bhùrn-luaidh a chaitheadh air."

Dh'fharraid i sin dè an dòigh air am faigheadh i na daoine fuadain air falbh, 's thuirt an seann duine rithe tilleadh dhachaigh, 's seasamh air an dùn aig doras an taighe 's glaodhach àird a cinn, trì uairean gun robh Dùn Bhurg na theine. Thigeadh a' chuideachd an sin a-mach le rèis a dh'fhaicinn an t-seallaidh iad fhèin 's dar gheibheadh i taobh a-mach an taighe iad 's an doras druidte orra, bha i ri car tuathail tarsainn no car-muiltein a chur 's a h-uile nì a bha iad ag obair leis. Thill i leis an fhiosrachadh a fhuair i, 's nar ràinig i an cnoc mu choinneamh an doras, ghlaodh i cho searbh 's cho cruaidh 's gun cluinneadh feadhainn a b' fhaid air astar na bha na beachd i "Tha teine an Dùn Bhurg! Dùn Bhurg ri theine! Dùn Bhurg na lasair dheirg!" Mun do chrìochnaich i an glaodh corranach, bha a' chuideachd-shìth a-mach às an taigh nan sradaichean, a' mùchadh 's a' saltairt air a chèile, feuch cò aca a bhiodh air thoiseach ann 's an "Holovohorhe" a bha aca a' ruigheachd an dorais 's iad ag èigheach:–

"Mo bhean 's mo phàistean
Mo chàise 's mo ghogan ime
Mo mhic 's mo nigheanan
'S mo chisteachan mòra mine
Mo chìr 's mo chàrdan
An snàmh 's a' chuigeal
Mo bhò 's a' bhuarach
'S na cuachan bainne
Eich 's na h-iallan
Cliabhan 's cinnean

'S an talamh 'cur roimhe
M' ùird 's m' innean
Dùn Bhurg ri theine
'S ma loisgear Dùn Bhurg
Loisgear mo mhùirn
'S mo mhireadh."

– h-uile aon a-riamh dhiubh a' caoidh rud a b' fheàrr 's a b' fhiù leotha a chaidh fhàgail san Dùn.

Nar fhuair a' bhean-taighe gun robh iad taobh a-muigh an dorais, chaidh i a-staigh air an cùlaibh cho luath 's b' urrainn dhi 's dhùin 's chrann i an doras orra, 's mar a dh'earbar rithe, chuir i air aimhreidh a h-uile sian air an robh na daoine 's na mnathan còire ag obair. Thug i a' bhann far na cuibhle, chuir i car sa chuigeil, na càrdan còmhla an àite a bhith cas mu seach, cara-muiltein don bheart-fhighe, am bùrn-luaidh far an teine, 's mar sin a-sìos. 'S gann a bha i ullamh dhe seo 's i air tòiseachadh air deasachadh do mhuinntir an taighe na thill na Daoine Còire air ais ag iarraidh a-staigh 's ag èigheach:

"Ionnairidh mhòr mhaith, bhean an taighe, leig a-staigh sinn."

"Chan urrainn mi," ors ise, "'s mo làmhan san taois."

Sin ghlaoidh iad ris a' chuibhle: "Chuibheall mhaith, èirich 's fosgail an doras dhuinn."

"Ciamar a dh'fheudas mi," ors a' chuibheall, "'s mi gun bhann."

Rinn iad an sin diùrras ris a' chuigeil: "Chuigeal ullamh ealamh, fosgail an doras dhuinn."

"'S mise gun dèanadh," ors a' chuigeal, "mur biodh car annam."

Thuirt iad a-nis ris na càrdan an doras fhosgladh.

"Dhèanamaid-ne sin glè thoilichte nam biodh comas nan cas againn."

Thug iad sin an aire don bheart-fhighe 's nach diùltadh i iad. Thuirt a' bheart-fhighe gun dèanadh mur biodh i cara-muiltein. Bhrìodail iad a-nis air a' bhùrn-luaidh an leigeil a-staigh ag ràdhainn ris."Bhùirn-luaidh, nach fhosgail thu 'n doras?"

"Chan urrainn mi 's mi far an teine," ors am bùrn-luaidh.

Bha iad thun toirt thairis 's a' fàs neo-fhoighidneach 's air a cheann mu dheire, thug iad an aghaidh, 's rinn iad an gearan ris a bhonnach bheag a' bha ga bhruich air leac an teintein 's thuirt iad ris:

"Bhonnaich bhig an àigh, fosgail an doras gu grad 's cabhag oirnn."

Dh'èirich am bonnach beag 's thug e an doras air cho luath 's a b' urrainn dha ach bha a' bhean-taighe na h-earalas. Air a dhèidhinn ghabh i 's rug i air 's thug i gòmag às 's an àite ruigheachd gu sneic an dorais, 's ann a thuit e na spleog air an ùrlar. Bho nach robh dòigh no dealbh tuilleadh aca air faighinn a-staigh, ghabh iad le dùrachd an sàs am fear an taighe 's b' e a cheann a b' aon bhall-coise caol 's iomain dhaibh gus an àite a bhith trom an d' fhàs e cho aotrom ri iteag.

Mar nach gabhadh an hò-rò fulang na b' fhaide, chuimhnich a' bhean-taighe mar a dh'iarraidh oirre a dhèanamh leis a' bhùrn-luaidh 's thog i làn cuaiche 's thilg i thairis air fear an taighe e. Dhùisg esan gun dàil. Bha an t-àm aige. Dh'èirich e 's dh'fhosgail e an doras 's sguir an ùpraid.

On one occasion, in a by-gone time, the wife of a landholder or rich farmer was at night, as was the custom of thrifty housewives in those days, after her husband and household had gone to rest, preparing woollen cloth (*clò*) for their use. Being excessively wearied and fatigued with her labours, she sought an outlet for her feelings, and said:

"O that someone would come from land or sea, from far or near, to help me with the work of making this cloth."

She had no sooner spoken, than she heard a knocking at the door, and a voice calling to her in a strange language, what she knew meant:

"Tall Inary, good housewife, open the door to me, for so long as I have you'll get."

She rose, and when she opened the door a strange-looking woman, dressed in shaded green, entered the house, passed her, and sat down at the spinning-wheel. She was no sooner seated, than a louder knocking came, and a voice calling out the self-same words:

"Tall Inary, good housewife, open your door, you'll get so long as I have anything."

When the housewife answered, another weird woman came in, and took her place at the distaff, then a yet louder knocking and voice came, in the same way demanding admission, and proffering help. No sooner was the door opened, than another strange being passed in, and sat to card the wool. As soon as she began to work a still louder knocking came to the door, and also a voice shouting:

"Tall Inary, good housewife, open the door quickly, and so long as I have you'll get."

When the door was opened, another curious-looking woman of the same appearance and dress glided in, and seating herself, began wool-teazing. Then another followed, with even a louder din, and when she got in she began pulling wool. They now came faster and quicker, one after another of them, with an ever-increasing din and clatter, till the house was quite full of fairies, men and women, each at work, and now their labours began in good earnest, teazing, carding, pulling, and rolling, distaff, spinning-wheel, and weaver's shuttle plying quick and fast, while the fulling-water, boiling, was spilling over, and the whirr of the spinning-wheel, rasping of the cards, rustle of the distaff, and the thrum of the loom could be heard far off. The good housewife endeavoured to still the uproar, and get enough of meat prepared for them, until the sweat could be seen dripping from her face, and heard falling in big drops on the floor. But as the night advanced their rapacious appetite seemed only to keep pace with their labours, and the universe would not keep them in meat. At midnight she was ready to drop down from excessive toil. She then tried to waken the good man, but in vain, she might as well strive to rouse a mill-stone. He would neither move nor speak, let her shake him and shout at him as she might. When she was almost at her wits' end she thought of going for advice to a wise man in the town land. Leaving her unaccountable helpers eating her last baking of bread, she slipped away, and reaching the sage, told him all her troubles, and how her husband could not be wakened. He chid her for her thoughtlessness in having asked for uncanny help, and said to her:

"As long as you live, do not wish, ask, or pray for anything unwise or improper, in case you get your desire, and bring evils on yourself. The people have come, and you will not get quit of them by laboured talk. Your husband is under spells, and before he can be awakened, your undesirable visitors must be got out of the house, and part of the fulling-water sprinkled over him."

She then asked by what means she could get rid of the strangers, and the wise man told her to return home, stand on the hillock at her own door, and cry out as loud as she could three times: "Burg Hill is on fire!" The company would then rush out to see for themselves, and when she got them outside, she was to disarrange, reverse, overturn, and upset everything they had been working with. She returned with the knowledge given her, and when she reached the hillock before the door, she cried out, so fearful and loud that she could be heard by people further away than those it was meant for: "There is fire in Burg Hill! Burg Hill is on fire! Burg Hill is in red flames of fire!"

Before she had finished the last alarming warning, the Fay people rushed out of the house, crushing and trampling on each other in their eagerness to be foremost in the "Holovohorohe", and as they hurried to the door they cried:–

"My wife and little ones,
My cheese and butter-keg,
My sons and daughters,
My big meal chests,
My comb and wool-cards.
Thread and distaff,
Cow and fetter.
Horses and traces.
Harrows and hoard,
And the ground bursting.
My hammers and anvil,
Burg Hill is on fire;
And if Burg Hill is burnt,
My pleasant occupations
And merriments are gone."

– each of them in their turn crying for the articles most prized by them which had been left in the Fairy knowe.

When the good-wife saw that they were all out of the house, she went in quickly behind them, carefully shut and fastened the door, and, as she was told to do, deranged everything at which the Fairy company had been working. She took the band off the spinning-wheel, twisted the distaff the opposite way, put the wool-cards together instead of being contrary, turned the loom topsy-turvy, and took the fulling-water off the fire, etc., etc. She had hardly finished this work, and begun the family baking, when the Fairy company returned, knocking for admission, and calling out:

"Tall Inary, good housewife, let us in."

"That, I cannot," she answered, "my hands are in the dough measure."

They then called to the Spinning-wheel: "Good Spinning-wheel, get up and open the door to us."

"How can I," said the Spinning-wheel, "when I am without a band?"

They now appealed to the Distaff: "Ready, quick Distaff, open the door for us."

"I would willingly open the door for you," said the Distaff, "but I am twisted contrary."

Then they asked the Wool-cards to open the door.

"We would do as you wish with pleasure, but we are foot-bound," said the Cards.

They now thought of the Weaving-loom, that it could not refuse them. The Weaving-loom said that it would, were it not that it was topsy-turvy. They now besought the Fulling-water to let them in, saying: "Fulling-water, will you not open the door?"

"I cannot, when I am off the fire," said the Fulling-water.

They were getting exhausted and impatient, and as a last resource they turned and made their complaint to the little Bannock that was toasting on the hearth, and said to it:

"Little Bannock of good fortune, open the door quickly, for we are in haste."

The little Bannock rose and sped to the door as fast as he could, but the good housewife was too alert for him. She ran after, caught and nipped him, so that instead of reaching the latch of the door he fell with a splatch on the floor. There being now no other way or means of getting in, they attacked the good-man of the house with such vehemence, that they made his head, with their cries to get in, from being heavy, as light and indifferent as a featherweight or light ball to the slenderest-footed football or shinty player.

When the hubbub became unbearable the good housewife remembered what she was told to do with the fulling-water. She lifted a cog-full and threw it over the good man, who awoke immediately. It was high time for him. He rose, opened the door, and the uproar ceased.

J. W.

Note.– A well-known and widely spread tale. This is the particular version summarised by Campbell, *Tales of the West Highlands*, vol. ii, p. 52. Campbell mentions several Highland variants. One from Lewis, "with curious variations unfit for printing." It is to be hoped that this version is not lost, as there is reason to believe it would throw much light upon the original form of the story. Mr. Hector McLean, Campbell's well-known assistant in collecting, has communicated a fragmentary version to the editor of this version. In the *Revue Celtique*, vol. iii, p. 181 et seq., Mr. David Fitzgerald prints in full or summarises five Irish versions from Limerick, Cork, Kerry, and Galway. P. Kennedy, *Fictions of the Irish Celt*, p. 164, prints a version much distorted and contaminated by witchcraft belief. Lady Wilde also gives a version in her *Ancient Legends of Ireland* (reprinted in Mr. Yeats' *Fairy and Folk Tales of the Irish Peasantry*, p. 165 et seq). The Scotch versions differ from the Irish ones in that in the latter the supernatural guests are unbidden. The present version is the only one which contains the incident of the Bannock. In none of the Irish versions do the fairy visitors obtain the food they ask for, the mortal is always instructed first how to get rid of them.

ALFRED NUTT.

THE FAIRIES' HILL

There is a green hill above Kintraw, known as the Fairies' Hill, of which the following story is told.

Many years ago, the wife of the farmer at Kintraw fell ill and died, leaving two or three young children. The Sunday after the funeral the farmer and his servants went to church, leaving the children at home in charge of the eldest, a girl of about ten years of age. On the farmer's return the children told him their mother had been to see them, and had combed their hair and dressed them. As they still persisted in their statement after being remonstrated with, they were punished for telling what was not true. The following Sunday the same thing occurred again. The father now told the children, if their mother came again, they were to inquire of her why she came. Next Sunday, when she reappeared, the eldest child put her father's question to her, when the mother told them she had been carried off by the "Good People" (Daoine Sìth), and could only get away for an hour or two on Sundays, and should her coffin be opened it would be found to contain only a withered leaf. The farmer, much perplexed, went to the minister for advice, who scoffed at the idea of any supernatural connection with the children's story, ridiculed the existence of "Good People", and would not allow the coffin to be opened. The matter was therefore allowed to rest. But, some little time after, the minister, who had gone to Lochgilphead for the day, was found lying dead near the Fairies' Hill, a victim, many people thought, to the indignation of the Fairy world he had laughed at.

Supplied by MRS. ANNIE THORPE, *née* MISS MACDOUGALL of *Lunga, Ardbecknish, Loch Awe.*

THE SKULL IN SADDELL CHURCH[8] AND THE SERVING GIRL[9]

The farmer living above a place named Barr had become aware that an attachment had sprung up between his son and the serving girl in his house, and he had long been meditating how to frustrate the designs of these two, and had pondered how he might get the girl away, and put an end to the love-affair. One winter's night, when the great flakes of snow came, driven by a furious tempest against the windows of the comfortable farm-house, and when all the family were gathered round the fire, he bethought him of the skull which was always kept in Saddell Church. This skull, the emblem of mortality, had been kept, time immemorial, in a conspicuous place, to remind the congregation that death was ever hovering about and inevitable. The farmer thought that he would make a proposition which the girl's love would not be strong enough to entertain, and that she would evade the test that he proposed to himself to make. The wind howled louder than ever, and the snowflakes fell faster and thicker, but this in no way altered the man's determination, and turning to her, he said, "If before the day breaks you bring me the skull that is in Saddell Church, you shall have my son for your husband."

Without a moment's hesitation, the poor girl made ready to face the awful storm and the driving snow, her faith and true love proof alike to the darkness and eeriness of the expedition. She never hesitated for a moment, however, and drawing her plaid over and round her pretty head, she made for the church in the teeth of the furious gale.

Old tales told in her childhood came back to her as she battled against the storm: tales such as are common to every land, and at times she half feared she might not have the courage to go through

---

8 Saddell is one of the "sacred places" of the Romish Church.

9 See *Hist. of Kintyre*, by Peter Mcintosh, published by R. Wilson, Jun., Campbelltown, MDCCCLXX.

the task. She stepped over the low wall of God's-acre, and found the door of the church standing wide open. The snow had covered the old tombs outside, and was drifting wildly into the church through the door, and her heart sank as she heard the wild rush of invisible creatures, which came apparently from all parts of the church. Again the tales of childhood crowded in on her mind, and her heart seemed to stand still, for the rushing and mysterious sounds continued, and could be heard above the shriek of the wind. Summoning up all her courage, she groped her way to the place where the skull was, and she took it in her arms and made her way out of the church. The same eerie, rushing sounds were repeated on all sides of her, and glad and thankful was she when she stood once more safe at the door of the farm, with the proud knowledge that she had won the lad of her heart, and that the farmer would now bless their union.

The farmer could scarcely believe his eyes when the girl showed him the skull. He thought no human being, much less a girl, would have shown so much courage, and he sent men to ascertain if the skull was indeed that which had been in Saddell Church. These arrived, and found the door had been somehow opened by the wind, and that a herd of deer had taken refuge in the church to be out of the violence of the storm. The farmer became convinced that the girl did truly love his son, and he no longer opposed their union, and the marriage shortly afterwards took place, amid great rejoicing, to the satisfaction of all true lovers.

TRADITIONS OF THE BRUCE

RELATED DY PETER MACINTOSH, ESQ.

———

The Bruce and the Goat.

In the year 1306, when Bruce was in Kintyre, a large reward being offered for his head by the English, the King came to the hill called Sliabh Gaoil, and being wearied with his flight, having been exposed to many hardships, he lay down at night-time on the side of this desolate hill. While lying thus, cold and hungry, it is said that a goat came and lay down by the King's side, keeping him warm with the heat of her body, and affording him nourishment also. In grateful remembrance of this he made a law that no goat should be poinded. On the following morning he supped in the same fashion as did the ninth Earl of Argyll in much later years, when pursued by the Athol men. On the road he encountered a poor beggar, the King, driven to extremity by hunger, asked him what he had, to which the beggar answered that he had but a little barley-meal about him. The King joyfully took some that was offered, and when he had come to a spring he took off his shoe and made a "crowdy", or stir-about, in the heel of the shoe, repeating as he did so these words:

"Is maith an còcair' an t-acras,

'S mairg nì talach air a' bhiadh,

Fuarag eòrn' à beul mo bhròige

An lòn as fheàrr a fhuair mi riamh."

Which signifies: "Hunger is a good cook, it is bad to slight food, barley-meal brose, out of my shoe, the best food I ever used."

For days the Earl of Argyll partook of the same dinner eaten out of his shoe, saying it was the sweetest dish he had ever tasted.[10]

The Bruce and General Douglas.

When Bruce drew near the Wood of Dunlaradh, near to Saddell in Kintyre, having come by Carradale, at a lonely spot he encountered a man, and inquired what his name was[11], the same question was put to the King, probably in a tone far from friendly, for neither would reply to the questions put, and, taking swords in hand, they commenced a furious hand-to-hand combat. So even was the fight, so expert were both swordsmen, that no result took place, and both were greatly out of breath. They renewed the combat, and again they were obliged to desist to get breath, so exhausted were both, and they sat down to rest themselves. The King said that it was but sad work, and no good purpose could be served by the death of either, and said, "Tell me your name, and I will tell you mine, I am Robert Bruce." "I agree," said the strange man, "I am General Douglas." The late foes kissed each other, and embraced, casting aside their swords. A great reward had been offered for the head of General Douglas also by the English Government. Thus ended the hard fight in the lonely wood near Saddell.

---

[10] See *Records of Argyll*. The Earl, pursued by Athol men, hides in a cleft of the rock in Glenshira.

[11] It may be noted that in these rude days to ask the name of a person was often the signal for a fight. It was considered cowardice to answer, and there are several records of fights taking place between septs from this cause.

The Stag-haunted Stream

In the ages gone by, when chiefs were wont to seek for fame, glory, and, perchance, wealth in foreign climes, a great man departed from the Western land, bound on some such errand. His noble wife, six years before, had left him a widower, she having been stricken with a terrible plague which raged throughout the land. Their only child, Morag, survived, and she was her father's joy. "Where," said he, "can I leave my child when I quit my home for a time?" After having thought over this matter, he recollected his kinsman, Fillan More, and he decided to leave his daughter under the shelter of his roof, where she would be watched over by his wife, and cheered by his happy household, there, thought he, she will grow in stature and in mind, and acquire all necessary feminine accomplishments, and grow into a vigorous woman. He noticed that there was a pallor on her cheek, not usual in a Highland girl, and that her gait lacked the elasticity of perfect health. No sooner had he thought the matter out than he acted on the decision arrived at, and he wrote to his kinsman, and all was arranged for the reception of Morag. She parted in sorrow from her father, but he assured her it was not for long, and was able to inspire some feeling of comfort in the poor child's heart, for child she was, as yet being but thirteen years of age when this took place, Morag soon became as one of the family. She joined both boys and girls in all their amusements, and before many months were over she was the picture of a healthy, happy girl.

Time slipped away. Years passed without her father returning, though Morag often heard of his ever-increasing prosperity, and of his many noble and daring deeds.

The two sons, Dermid and Cailean, were Morag's devoted slaves, and would encounter any peril to procure for her the accomplishment of her wishes, and, as might be expected, before either of them were aware of it, the hearts of both the young fellows were given to Morag.

She was now in her seventeenth year, and of surpassing beauty of form and disposition. It was long before she realised that for either of them she had other than sisterly love, but circumstances occurred causing Dermid to unburden his heart and speak of his feelings, and poor Morag felt she could have sympathised with his brother had he approached with such words.

It was the old tale, so often to be renewed, of the course of true love seldom running smooth, and in this case it ended in a dire calamity.

The subject came up, and a bitter quarrel took place. The first tragedy that darkened the world was again to be repeated. There, on the mountain-side lay Cailean, slain by his brother, the heather and the moss dyed crimson with his life-blood. And Morag! who can portray her feelings? She wept and wept, until her tears formed a stream down the side of Ben Cruachan, and from its waters her lover reappeared in the form of a stag, which may to this day be seen near that water in the early hours of autumnal mornings.

From MRS. CAMPBELL *of Dunstaffnage,*
née MISS CAMPBELL *of Monzie.*

The Questions put by Finn to the Maiden,

And her Answers

---

1. "What is more numerous than the grass?" said Finn (Fionn).

   "The dew-drops," said the maiden.

2. "What is whiter than the snow?" said Finn.

   "Truth," said the maiden.

3. "What is loveliest of hue?" said Finn.

   "The bloom of childhood," said the maiden.

4. "What is hotter than fire?" said Finn.

   "The hospitable man's face when a stranger cometh and there is nothing to offer him," said the maiden.

5. "What is swifter than the wind?" said Finn.

   "The mind of a woman," said the maiden.

6. "What is sharper than a sword?" said Finn.

   "A woman's wit between two men," said the maiden.

7. "What is bitterer than poison?" said Finn. "The reproach of an enemy," said the maiden.

8. "What is blacker than the raven?" said Finn.

   "Death," said the maiden.

9. "What is best for a hero?" said Finn.

   "High deeds and humble pride," said the maiden.

10. "What is best for a woman?" said Finn. "Generous tenderness," said the maiden.

11. "What is softer than down?" said Finn. "The palm[12] of the cheek," said the maiden.

12. "What is best of jewels?" said Finn. "A knife," said the maiden.

Note.– Compare Campbell, *Popular Tales*, vol. iii, pp. 36-37. There are instructive variations between the two versions. Nos. 3 and 10 are not in Campbell. In No. 4 the question in Campbell runs: "What is redder than blood?" whilst Campbell gives as the answer to "What is hotter than fire? – A woman's reasoning betwixt two men," which certainly does not seem right. On the other hand, Campbell gives: "A woman's thought between two men," as the answer to our No. 5. I am inclined to think this is more correct than our version. See the tale of Michael Scott, and my note, *supra*, pp. 31-34. Our No. 9 runs thus in Campbell: "What deed is the best of deeds? – A high deed and low conceit," which may be more moral, but is not as delightfully characteristic of the Highland temperament as our version. Campbell has about half as many riddles again as our version, but only one is of great interest: "What is it will not bide lock and chain? – The eye of a man about his friend, it will not brook shutting or holding, but looking on him." In Campbell the maiden is Gràinne, Finn's wife, and Mr. Hector MacLean cites the tradition that he married her, as she was the only woman who could answer all his questions.

ALFRED NUTT.

---

12 "Palm" is here used as the down on the cheek.

THE

WAR DRESS OF THE CELT

It is curious to reflect that, in the days of Charles I, the Highland chiefs still wore the quilted war garb which was seen by the great German artist of Nuremberg, Albert Dürer.

The big two-handed sword was still used in Carolian days. The shorter one-handed basket-hilted sword was in use throughout the '45, but they clung long to the true Highland weapon, the two-handed sword.

Their steel helmets – chain-mail, and often their targes (but not always) – swords, and greaves were of native manufacture. The helmet decidedly belonged to no other land. The two-handed sword varied from that used by the Norwegians and Swiss in pattern and detail of make. The weakest arm of the Celt was the bow-and-arrow,[13] for it is often noted that the archers of England and of other countries greatly excelled them. It is noteworthy that the bow-and-arrow seldom appears on the finest of the tombstones, but it does appear on various sculptures of a rude and early type, it, however, is never placed prominently forward, as is the case with the sword, the targe, and the spear, these being their favourite weapons.

The war dress of no Asiatic or European corresponds exactly with that of the Celt.

Quilted war coats were worn up to recent days by the Japanese, but no dress among all the wondrous variety of war garb is similar to that used of old by the Celtic people.

---

13 "We find the Irish highly appreciated the arrow made by the Highlanders, and that they were in great request. The Island of Islay was famous for the manufacture of sword-guards,"

The kilt of the 16th century, worn very full and standing out well from the hip, in use in Germany and France, comes somewhat near, but, as a glance at the figures of the knights will show, does not tally. The Celt stands alone in singularity of dress.

IRISH SOLDIERS

From Albert Dürer's Drawing

TOMB OF KNIGHT, CHURCHYARD, KILNINIAN, ORONSAY

From William Galloway's Drawing

ORNAMENT ON CUFF OF RIGHT SLEEVE OF LARGEST EFFIGY, ORONSAY PRIORY

EMBROIDERY ON CUFF OF GAUNTLETS, LEFT SLEEVE, KNIGHT'S TOMB, ORONSAY PRIORY

From William Galloway's Drawings

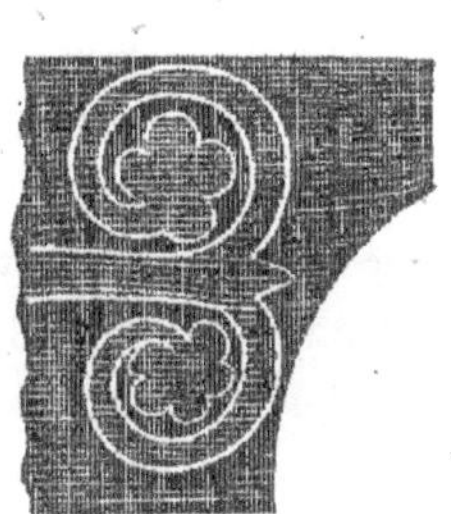

TERMINAL OR SIDE DETAIL OF SCROLL ON KNIGHT'S GAUNTLET CUFF, SMALLER EFFIGY, ORONSAY PRIORY

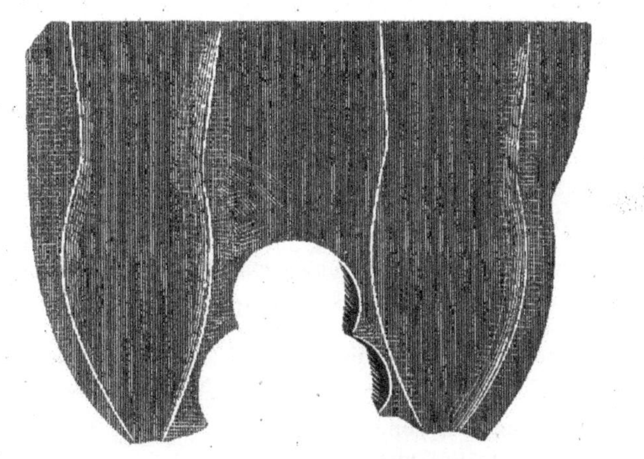

TERMINATION OF FEET, KNIGHT'S TOMB, ORONSAY PRIORY

From William Galloway's Drawings

Celtic Military Dress.

Albert Dürer, born 1471, died 1528, has drawn and coloured Irish military dress of the 16th century with an accuracy that leaves nothing to be desired. These men, without the shadow of a doubt, he drew from the life, the detail of dress, moreover, corresponds with what is sculptured, on the tombstones of Western Scotland. The ever-recurring two-handed sword is here given, and the long, saffron-coloured and quilted garb, which, as regards the Western Highland knights, was worn kilted a little shorter, is amply illustrated in his beautiful drawing.

The Bascinet is peculiar, and differs from the Scottish form, it appears to have had a sliding-bar, or guard, which could be lowered to protect the nose from a sword-blow, as have the Indian helmets – another instance of Eastern forms adopted by the Western nations. The quick eye of that excellent antiquary, Mr. William Galloway, enables us to know even the detail of needlework embroidered on the war-dresses of the knights of old. Those who know what havoc rain, frost, and snow are slowly making on the recumbent effigies of the Western Isles, will appreciate the care taken to record minute details such as these, which must soon inevitably perish and be lost for ever.

Some few years back, there were some Celtic authorities who thought that the legs of the Scottish knights were represented as being bare on the Scottish tombstones, but this is not at all usually intended, or, indeed, the case. The sharp shin-ridge of the greaves proves that the legs of the knights are encased in plate armour, and on a tomb on Oronsay the spur straps are elaborated.

On a tombstone on Inishail, Loch Awe, now deplorably defaced, a few years back it was easy to make out the long plumes depending from the conical helmets of the two men-at-arms supporting the shield. The plumes descended to, and lower than, the shoulders.

When last seen this was much obliterated by the action of the weather. The owner of this island, the Duke of Argyll, has sanctioned steps being taken for the better preservation of this grave and other tombstones here found, and these are being carried out under the eyes of H.R.H. the Princess Louise, Marchioness of Lorne.

It would be impossible to write on the war dress of the Celtic knights without referring to the labours of the late Mr. H. D. Graham, who was long on the Island of Iona, and who drew the whole of the more important monuments and tombstones there to be found. The quilted dress and the plate or chain-armour portions differ slightly, but on the whole all indicate the same military garb, which garment was in vogue long after the days of Albert Dürer.

Illustrations of these types are given, and in so doing we must go to the work published some years back by Mr. Graham, whose drawings are of all the greater value, inasmuch as a great deal of what he was able readily to delineate is now greatly effaced by the action of time and stormy weather. In the year 1636 this quilted garb appears on a tomb of one of the Macleans.

The late Mr. Graham reminds us that, as regards the exact date to which the monumental tombs and slabs can be attributed, it is well to remember that only *after* the time of the Bruce *do dates appear*, and that dates anterior to, and during, his reign do not appear on tombs or on charters.[14]

The tomb of one of his greatest friends, Innes or Angus og (young Angus), namely, that of Macdonald of Islay and Kintyre (Plate X, in Mr. H. D. Graham's work), is a fine example of foliated pattern commencing from four lions or leopards, whose tails blossom into a pattern of great beauty. Above all is the galley with the sail furled. The inscription is as follows: "Hie jacet corpus Angusii filii Domini Angusii MacDomnill de Ila." We can infer the

---

[14] H.D. Graham's *Antiquities of Iona.*

date of others from this example of lettering and of execution of sculpture.

The Macleans[15] are mentioned in the Craignish tales, and the garb worn by these warriors is therefore given. No clan showed a more warlike spirit than that of Maclean. The breath of their nostrils was the breath of battle.

---

15 On the authority of Maclaine of Lochbuie, we find the name thus variously spelt in Lochbuie Papers: Maclayne, McLean, Maclain, McLain, McLeane, Macllean, Mclain, Maclaine, Maclean. – Ed.

TOMB OF MACLEAN OF COLL, IONA

TOMB OF MACLAINE OF LOCHBUIE, IONA

Red Hector of the Battles commands as Lieut.-General under Earl Ross at the battle of Harlaw, 1411. Hector 9th Duart falls fighting at the head of his clan at Flodden. Hector 16th falls fighting at Inverkeithing.

Their hearts beat loudest and most joyously amid the carnage of the battle, with them a peaceful death-bed was held in contempt, or as a great misfortune. To them the blast of the trumpet and the shock of battle were more familiar than the sounds and scenes of home life and peaceful days. In the last great rising of the clans they are said to have presented the most splendid and warlike appearance, headed by their various chiefs. Perhaps some day in some great battle in the New World "the Children of the Mist" will yet once again be gathered together to emulate the deeds done of old, for in America, Australia, or New Zealand alone, perhaps, could Highland brigades be easily got up in war time – so depopulated are many districts in our time.

Among others whose dust lies in Iona is that of Ailean nan Sop[16] and Cairnburg. Besides the murder of the Laird of Torloisg, perpetrated by Ailean nan Sop, one other incident must be named.

Right in the throat of a violent current rises the fortress-island of Cairnburg, which "for a thousand years" was a royal garrison. This island has precipitous sides, and is of volcanic origin, as is the case with the other islands lying off the coast of Mull. It lies midway between the Treisinnis isles and the mainland, and is said to have been fortified by one of the kings of Norway.

Maclean of Gigha, better known by the name of Ailean nan Sop, nearly lost his life at this place in the following manner. A daughter of "Barra" was on a visit to the Macleans, the father and mother of Ailean had gone to the mainland, and Ailean, who had conceived a violent passion for the girl, found that his love met no response,

---

16 i.e., Allan of the wisps of straw. He was so called because, in burning houses, he used, with his own hands, to set wisps of straw up against them, and set fire to them.

irritated, he sought to do her a violence. The girl, rushing past the guard-house, hotly pursued by the young Maclean, made straight for the precipice, one of the servants who was witness to the intended violence followed, and as he seized the hand of the girl, he at the same time with his other hurled Ailean over the brow of the rock, a protruding ledge caught Ailean in his fall, but there he remained till he had asked pardon of the lady, and promised to pardon the servant who had rescued her. Before many years were gone this rough knight acted as ambassador on behalf of the Lord of the Isles to the English Court.

During the minority of Queen Mary, and at the time of the regency of the Lord of Arran, Ailean went to England with the Earl of Lennox, who was engaged in a treasonable conspiracy with the English king. Later on, Ailean obtained Queen Mary's pardon, and he was buried at Iona, and his image was carved on his tomb in full Celtic armour. The shelf on which Ailean fell is yet called "Uirigh Ailein nan Sop," *i.e.*, Ailean nan Sop's Couch.

The image with the flowing hair tombstone is remarkable for the long, flowing ringlets of the knight, which are represented escaping from under the helmet. The chiefs and inhabitants of the Isles during the 17th century wore the hair long, as did the Irish Celts.

TOMB OF MACLEAN OF DUART, IONA

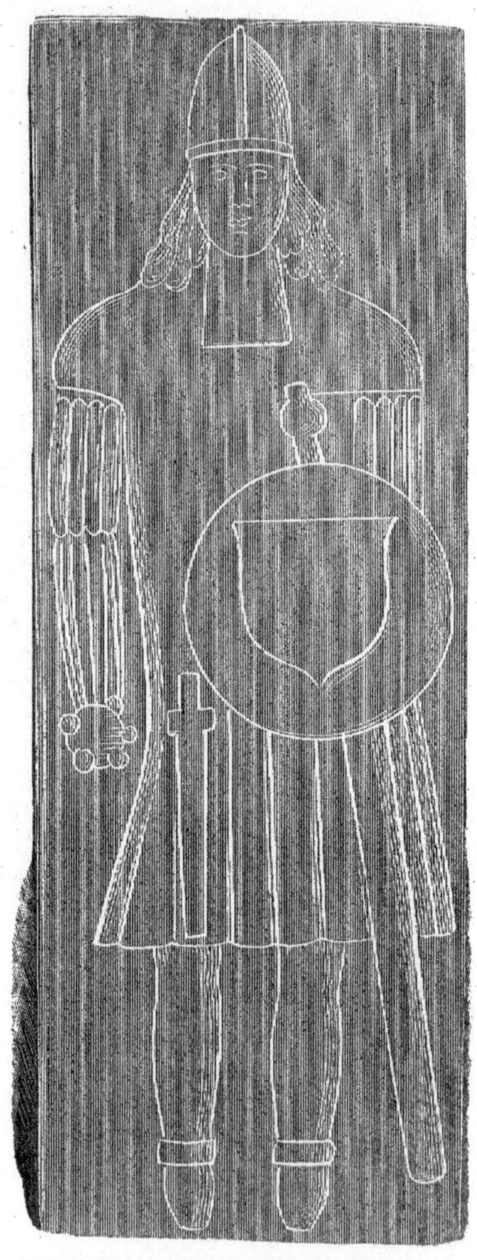

TOMB OF SIR ALLAN MACLEAN OF DUART
Douglas makes him 3rd Baronet of Morven. Died 1674, aged 38

TOMB OF MACLEAN OF ROSS, IONA

MACLEOD'S TOMB, IONA
Armed and kilted figure of the Knight in centre of stone

MACQUARRIE'S TOMB, IONA

It may be remembered that in Elizabethan days in Ireland it was lawful to kill a man wearing long hair, that being one of the characteristics by which the rebels were identified.

The cut representing the Irish Celtic soldiery,[17] 1599, at the time of the rebellion in attitudes in this plate leaving no doubt that this is one of the figures of an ancient war-dance now lost, much as the ancient sword-dance of the Highlands is also lost to memory and to practice.

The well-known long, hanging sleeves are admirably shown here in the right-hand figure of the group (proper right-hand). The whole of them are in those long, flowing garments which were worn also by the Highland Scottish Celts, and which so astounded Sir William Sacheverell in 1688, when he was in the Island of Mull, and of which he has given an account in a work published in London, 1702.

The figure wearing the helmet has a falling plume, which tallies with what has been carved on the tomb of one of the Highland chiefs, therefore this cut is trustworthy as to the detail.

---

[17] From Knight's *Hist. of England.*

The War Trumpet of Celtic Ireland.

It is not singular that the Irish, who excelled to such a degree in the manufacture of brooches and other ornaments, should take equal care in the manufacture of their war-trumpets of bronze. It puzzles the most expert manufacturer of our day to know how they made these same trumpets, so fine is the rivet-work. One of the greatest of Roman jewellers, now established in London, Mr. Giuliano, has furnished an explanation of the process employed by the ancient Irish.

The British Museum may in vain be ransacked for information as to how they riveted their splendid semi-circular war-horns. To Sir Denham Jephson Norreys are we indebted for a valuable paper on the manufacture of the Celtic trumpet, in the Royal Irish Academy, which appears in the *Proceedings and Papers of the Royal Archaeological Association of Ireland*, vol, iv. Part II, Fourth Series.

The Irish Knight O'More.

To Mr. Thomas O'Gorman are we indebted for a woodcut and an account of a tomb at Abbeyleix, Queen's County. As the tombs with effigies of knights are not so common in Ireland, it is worthwhile to reproduce this cut for comparison with the tombstone-figures found in Western Scotland, and in England, and elsewhere. The date is 1500.

Here is Mr. O'Gorman's account of the figure:

EFFIGY OF MELAGHLIN O'MORE, ABBEYLEIX,
QUEEN'S COUNTY, IRELAND

"In one of the gardens attached to the residence of Lord de Vesci, at Abbeyleix, in the Queen's County, there is preserved the top slab of an ancient tomb, having the figure of a warrior sculptured on it, of which the annexed woodcut gives some idea. An inscription in raised old English letters round the margin informs us that it was erected to a member of the O'More family, once the potent rulers of the surrounding district, but the inscription is in parts both imperfect and illegible, so that neither the date nor the exact position of the person commemorated can be given with certainty. Still, as it is one of the very few effigial monuments of our native chieftain houses anterior to the reign of Elizabeth remaining to us, a notice may be desirable. . . . .

"The following is a brief description of the armour exhibited, which very closely resembles that in use in England during the reign of Richard II (1377-99). On the head is the conical bascinet, but whether it had a vizor or not I cannot say (though I rather think it had not), as that part of the head, and also the face, is sadly mutilated, the neck and shoulders are covered by the camail or tippet of chain-mail, which droops down far on the breast, on the shoulders, and apparently lying over the camail, are protecting pieces of plate, similar to those on the elbows. The body is defended by overlapping plates or bars, from which descends a skirt of chain-mail covering the upper part of the thighs, or it may be the end of a shirt of mail lying under the body-armour. The thighs are also covered with overlapping bars, similar to those on the body, and there are knee-pieces, but these are rather indistinct. The arms are covered with plate, having elbow-pieces. The hands have gauntlets, but the feet and lower part of the legs appear to have had no protection, at least, there is no appearance of armour on them now.

As already stated, I cannot give the inscription which surrounds this figure in full. The words which are legible are at the beginning and at the end of it, and are as follows:
'Hic jacet Malaoas omora Filius Nia: . . . . . anno Dni MCCCCC :
: . . . cui aie ppiciet de am. . . .' "

The Armed Highlanders of the 17th and 18th Centuries, with Remarks on the Fighting Power and Strength of the Clans.

It was reserved to John Graham of Claverhouse – Claverhouse the incarnate, the ideal soldier of his day, on whose face and form women and men alike loved to gaze, whose life-long dream it was to emulate the Great Montrose, a man whose heart stood still at nothing, to whom no song nor chant equalled the music, the long-drawn reverberations of the fight, whose smoke of incense was the smoke of battle, whose only prayer to God was that he might fall in some great charge amid the "thunderous music and carnage of the battle" – to show the fighting strength of the Highlanders in one great and dramatic scene, memorable to this day, for few can gaze on the narrow pass of Killiecrankie without thinking of the charge of the clans, when the very hills appeared moving masses of colour. He knew well how, suddenly, to appear before the armed clans, and to persuade them to forego long-standing feuds and side with him: he knew how to convert the various streams of warlike passion, of ancient enmity and revenge, into one grand and mighty torrent of destruction with which he overwhelmed the Southern troops at the pass of Killiecrankie. He persuaded them to spend that hour with Dundee which has made the day so memorable.

It is a noteworthy fact that in the '45 era, Mr. Campbell of Stonefield, a reliable and high authority on such matters, placed the fighting strength of the Highlanders at *sixty thousand men*. It is not too much to assert that no other European country of an equal area could have shown so warlike or a finer fighting force.

Lightning Source UK Ltd.
Milton Keynes UK
UKHW010731070223
416609UK00002B/513

9 781907 165535